DEAR SANDY—

QUESTIONS ARE
THE ANSWER!

HAPPINESS
ALWAYS,

Bill May

The MAGIC
IN ASKING
THE Right Questions

Create your Destiny through Power Thinking

by

BILL MAYER

The Magic in Asking the Right Questions
Create your Destiny through Power Thinking

Bill Mayer International
11782 Alps Way
Escondido, CA 92026
Tel 760 • 751 • 2798
Fax 760 • 751 • 2799

Cover Design, Graphic Illustrations, and Production by
Bennett Peji Design – La Jolla, California
Art Director: Bennett Peji
Designers: Minka Willig
Chakra Kusuma
Illustrator: Rafael Lopez

ISBN 0-9656160-3-7

First Edition

Printed in the United States of America

ACKNOWLEDGMENTS

Betty and "Xie" Mayer (Mom and Dad),
> *for your unconditional love and support and for always being there for me.*

Mary-Ellen Drummond,
> *for providing a great role model and inspiring me to "reach for the stars."*

Susan Lipton, Barbara Hendrickson, and Becky Colgan,
> *whose editing skills and expertise helped me to express my thoughts more clearly.*

Bennett Peji,
> *whose emotion-evoking graphic design and creativity continue to amaze me.*

Nancy and Adelaide, my wife and daughter,
> *for always believing in me and for your love and encouragement.*

And finally, a special thank you to my mentors, coaches of wisdom, from whom I have learned many of life's lessons,
> *James Allen, Earl Nightingale, Napoleon Hill, Wayne Dyer, Brian Tracy, Denis Waitley, Ken Blanchard, Deepak Chopra, and Tony Robbins.*

Dedication

TO MY SON, BILLY,
and
TO ALL FUTURE GENERATIONS
of
POWER THINKERS

CONTENTS

$\mathcal{I}$CON - TENTS

MAYERISM: Key Concept

POWER THINKING QUESTION

WARM WISHES and HAPPINESS

SUMMARY: Section/Chapter

$\mathcal{I}$NTRODUCTION

Ever since I can remember, I've been searching for answers about life. I asked a lot of Why? and What's it all about? type questions. I was intrigued by human behavior and wondered why some people were happy and successful and others were not.

As a fifteen-year-old high-school sophomore, I was in the top one percent of my class academically. I was captain of my soccer, basketball, and tennis teams, yet I was insecure and unhappy. Why? I couldn't figure it out, but these circumstances triggered my lifelong search for answers.

After twenty-five years of searching, reading hundreds of books, and attending countless seminars, I found that all trails led to one basic conclusion: Ninety-nine percent of who you are and who you will become is determined by your thoughts. The origins of your self-esteem, your happiness, your integrity, your character, your prosperity, your sense of purpose, your "everything" can all be traced to your thoughts.

I realized that if my thoughts control my life and who I am, then if I could learn to control my thoughts, I could control my life and destiny. To control my thoughts, I had to first define thinking. Thinking is essentially an internal conversation you have with yourself. More specifically, it is an ongoing series of questions and answers within your mind.

I concluded that the quality of my life is determined by the quality of my thinking. The quality of my thinking is determined by the quality of the questions I ask myself on a daily basis. So the secret to a better life is to continually ask myself better questions!

In this book I will show you how you can have almost anything you want in life if you ask yourself enough of the right questions.

The Magic in Asking the Right Questions is based on the concept of *Power Thinking*. Power Thinking is taking responsibility for your own thinking and striving to improve the quality of your thoughts by consistently asking yourself empowering questions. Applying this question-asking technique can positively transform your life. This book will teach you how to master this highly effective skill.

Power Thinking is also about choices – thought choices. Power Thinking recognizes a human being's unique ability to choose what he or she thinks about. Do you choose happy or depressed thoughts? Affluent or needy thoughts? Trustworthy or dishonest thoughts?

Power Thinking gives you direction, taps into your creativity, and encourages self-worth and a cheerful disposition. It is a way of thinking that is positive, healthy, loving, appreciative, flexible, focused, and action- and abundance-oriented.

Power Thinking emphasizes living consciously – in the now and enjoying the moment. It encourages developing the skill to live more consciously – in the present time. This is the only way you can choose to change any of your negative, often unconscious, thinking patterns.

Power Thinking starts with the first thought you have when you awake and finishes with your last thought before you go to sleep.

If you want to improve the quality and direction of your life, then you must change and improve the quality of your thoughts. For anyone, Power Thinking offers a reasonable solution. For me, Power Thinking is the answer.

Good luck on your personal growth journey through Power Thinking. May this adventure empower you to be exactly who you want to be, to do all that you dream to do, and to have everything you wish to have.

Written with love, respect, and encouragement,

Bill Mayer

CHAPTER 1

Control Your Thoughts, Control Your Destiny

The only thing
over which you have absolute control
is your own thoughts.
It is this that puts you in a position
to control your own destiny.

PAUL G. THOMAS

OUTCOMES OF THOUGHTS

Thinking is the highest function of a human being! Over the years, thinking has been a topic discussed and argued by many of the world's greatest philosophers, prophets, and teachers. There has consistently been a common denominator among these great minds, supporting one universally accepted truth. This was communicated succinctly by Napoleon Hill, author of *Think and Grow Rich*. He said, **"You become what you think about."** The following select group of wise men concurred with this belief.

As you believe, so shall it be done unto you.
JESUS

A man's life is
what his thoughts make of it.
MARCUS AURELIUS

A man is what he thinks about
all day long.
RALPH WALDO EMERSON

A man is literally what he thinks.
JAMES ALLEN

What you believe to be yourself,
you are.
CLAUDE M. BRISTOL

An important fundamental belief of Power Thinking is that, in fact, you do become what you think about. These words, when understood and applied, are extremely powerful. Why are they so significant?

Δ *Your thoughts control your life (destiny).*

Δ *You can control your thoughts.*

Δ *You can control your destiny.*

The greatest "truths" are often the most simple. This is no exception. Control your thoughts, and you will control your destiny.

The direction you go and the results you get in your life no longer have to be determined by external circumstances. Controlling and managing your internal thoughts will take you in the direction you want to go and help you to create the destiny you desire.

Every one of your thoughts and subsequent actions are going to have an effect in your life. **Who you are at this moment is the result of all your thoughts in your life thus far. In fact, all causation is mental – everything originates with thought.** You can clearly see this concept in the following illustration.

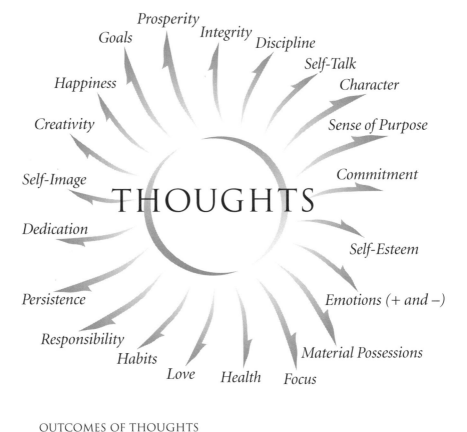

OUTCOMES OF THOUGHTS

I believe that all things ever created by man can trace their origins to a conscious or unconscious thought.

If you combine this belief with the understanding that most individuals have a minimum of 50,000 thoughts per day, then you can see how developing the skill to control and guide your thoughts becomes invaluable.

How do you control your thoughts? You control your thoughts through questions – the questions you ask yourself on a daily basis.

△ *Thinking is the highest function of a human being.*

△ *You become what you think about.*
- *Your thoughts control your destiny.*
- *You can control your thoughts.*
- *You can control your destiny.*

△ *You control your thoughts through the questions you ask yourself.*

CHAPTER 2

There is Magic in
Asking the Right Questions

I had six honest serving men
who taught me all I knew;
their names were What and Where and When
and Which and Why and Who.

RUDYARD KIPLING

WHERE'S THE MAGIC?

The magic is in the mysterious power of questions, which produces extraordinary results. In an instant, by stimulating your "mind's genie" with the right question, you can magically and immediately change your emotional state from negative to positive.

How you feel is determined by what you focus on, and what you focus on is determined by the questions you ask yourself. If you want to "magically" feel better, simply ask yourself better questions.

The secret to living a happier, more positive, emotionally enriched life is to learn to control your mental focus by developing, practicing, and mastering the skill of *asking the right questions.*

THE RIGHT QUESTIONS

Asking the right questions is a unique skill that can be developed, improved, and eventually mastered with practice. It is the single most important skill in shaping your destiny. The quality of your life will be determined by the quality of the questions you ask yourself.

How do you determine the *right* questions to ask yourself? To answer this, it is important to understand that *emotionally speaking*, there are primarily three types of questions:

1. **Disempowering Questions (DQs).** This type of question, when answered, will inevitably trigger a *negative* emotion causing unhappiness, anger, anxiety, or depression and will make you feel miserable.

   "Why did this have to happen to me?"
   Your mind is *guided* toward a negative response as a result of the unfavorable implications of this question. Your mind will first come up with answers it's familiar with by sorting through your memory bank. It also has the capacity to create some imaginary reasons, feeling just as real and just as painful, if you continue to ask the same disempowering question. With each answer you will feel more unhappy, angry, anxious, or depressed.

2. **Neutral Questions (NQs).** This type of question, when answered, will elicit no emotional response.

    "What channel is Jeopardy on?"

    "How much is two plus two?"

    "What is your name?"

3. **Empowering Questions (EQs).** This type of question, when answered, will stimulate *positive* emotions such as happiness, serenity, or creativity and will help you feel more joyful and content.

    "What kind of work would I love to do?"

    Your mind is directed to come up with positive responses as a result of the favorable implications of this question. The more specific you are with the questions you ask, the more you can control and direct your thoughts, and thus your life, in the positive direction you want it to go.

    "What kind of work would I love to do,

    that would provide a tremendous service,

    earn a minimum of $10,000 per month,

    and I could have fun doing it?"

Of these three types of questions, Power Thinkers concern themselves with the disempowering and the empowering ones, since these two elicit the most emotional response. You want to eliminate the DQs which are negative and destructive. You want to reinforce the EQs which are positive and constructive. Therefore, when you refer to "the magic in asking the right questions," the **right questions are the empowering ones.**

More specifically, the right questions are the questions that, when answered and acted upon, will lead you to your **desired outcome**. There are primarily three types of desired outcomes. They are the desired states of

1. **Being** – such as feeling happy or being energetic
2. **Doing** – such as playing the piano or traveling to Europe
3. **Having** – such as buying a new car or owning your home

The right questions, when answered, will lead you to any one or any combination of the above desired outcomes. There is often an overlap. For example, playing the piano (doing) might very well make you feel happy (being).

The right questions are the empowering ones because their desirable outcomes will put you in a positive emotional state. Subconscious, automatic, robot-like questions are often of a negative, disempowering nature, so they often do not fit into the "right question" category. In fact most, if not all, of the process of asking the right questions is done on a conscious, present-time plane of thought. Therefore, learning to consciously control the questions you ask yourself is one of the most important skills you must develop and master to reach your ultimate destiny.

The quality of your life is determined by the quality of the questions you ask yourself. Remember – you can have almost anything you want in life if you ask yourself enough of the right questions.

THE FIVE A'S
OF ASKING AWARENESS

How do you develop the skill of asking the right questions? Simply ask yourself, "Are the questions I'm asking myself taking me in the direction I want to go with my life? Are they taking me to my desired outcome?" If your answer is "Yes" – great! If your answer is "No" – then **ask yourself better, more empowering questions!**

To ensure a successful result when asking an empowering question, utilize the Five A's of Asking Awareness. This is a question-asking cycle that, when understood and applied to completion, will guarantee that you can have almost anything your want in life if you ask enough of the right questions. It is essentially a success formula for your step-by-step application and follow-through after asking yourself an empowering question. The Five A's of Asking Awareness are Ask, Answer, Act, Acknowledge, and Adjust. Refer to the following illustration to clarify this empowering question-asking cycle.

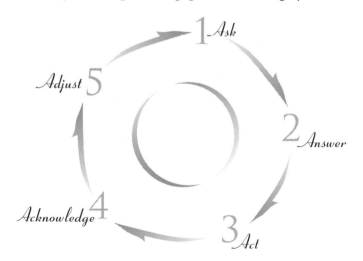

ASKING AWARENESS CYCLE

EXPLANATION OF
ASKING AWARENESS CYCLE

First, establish your desired outcome by simply asking your-self, "What is my desired outcome?" Then apply the Five A's of Asking Awareness.

1. *Ask – An empowering question that will lead you to your desired outcome.*

2. *Answer – Your question.*

3. *Act – Take action on your answer. The hallmark of Power Thinkers is their ability to act immediately and decisively.*

4. *Acknowledge – Where you are. Has this action taken you to your desired outcome? If yes, great! If no, then adjust.*

5. *Adjust – Simply ask a better, more specific question and repeat the Five A's of Asking Awareness.*

Sylvia asked herself, "What is my desired outcome?" Her response was, "I want to speak Spanish fluently within a year." Sylvia made this decision in January and began to apply the Five A's of Asking Awareness. Chronologically, this is what her progress toward her desired outcome looked like:

JANUARY 15

1. *Ask – "What's the best way to start learning Spanish?"*

2. *Answer – Get a beginners' book on how to speak Spanish.*

3. *Act – Sylvia spent one hour a day reading and studying beginning Spanish.*

4. Acknowledge – "Has this taken me to my desired outcome? No, but I am making some progress."

5. Adjust – Ask a better, more specific question.

MARCH 1

1. Ask – "How can I speed up the learning process?"

2. Answer – Get a Spanish home-study course on audio tapes.

3. Act – Sylvia used her car as a "traveling university" and listened to tapes an hour every weekday for over two months.

4. Acknowledge—"Has this taken me to my desired outcome? No, but I'm halfway there."

5. Adjust – Ask a better, more specific question.

MAY 15

1. Ask – "How can I apply the knowledge I've learned in a more conversational mode?"

2. Answer – Sign up for a class where the instructor and students speak only Spanish.

3. Act -Sylvia enrolled in a ten-week intensive Spanish class through a local university and had perfect attendance.

4. Acknowledge – "Has this taken me to my desired outcome? Almost, but I'm not quite where I want to be."

5. Adjust – Ask a better, more specific question.

AUGUST 1

1. Ask – "How can I get my Spanish speaking to be more natural?"

2. Answer – Go on a two-week educational trip to Cancun, Mexico with twelve other class members and the instructor on August 15.

3. *Act – Sylvia committed herself to speak only Spanish for the two weeks while she was in Cancun.*

4. *Acknowledge – "Has this taken me to my desired outcome? Yes, I'm speaking Spanish fluently and I'm even three months ahead of my desired outcome timetable."*

5. *Adjust – End of cycle!*

There is no need for Sylvia to adjust because she has reached her desired outcome. The more you use the Five A's of Asking Awareness, the easier this question-asking cycle becomes.

The example of Sylvia was intentionally long and drawn out so that you could clearly see each step of the Asking Awareness Cycle. A much simpler everyday example is Hal and his turn to wash the evening dinner dishes. As you might suspect, Hal does not enjoy washing dishes.

Hal first established his desired outcome: "I want dish washing to be fun." Now, let's apply the Five A's of Asking Awareness:

1. *Ask – "How can I make it fun?"*

2. *Answer – "I can sing a fun, upbeat song while doing the dishes."*

3. *Act – Hal sings "I Feel Good" by James Brown and throws in a little improvised dancing as well.*

4. *Acknowledge – Hal asks himself, "Has this taken me to my desired outcome?" Yes! Hal is smiling and having fun.*

5. *Adjust – There is no need to adjust, since Hal has reached his desired outcome of having fun doing the dishes.*

If, at the Acknowledge stage, you don't reach your desired outcome, persist in applying an important Power-Thinking principle: **"If at first you don't succeed, then ask a better**

question." Remember that you can have almost anything you want in life if you ask yourself enough of the right questions.

If you implement the Five A's of Asking Awareness and continue to make *distinctions* by asking better questions as you go along, you will guarantee the success of realizing your desired outcome. It really does work! Your determined self-discipline and relentless perseverance will ensure this outcome.

Consistently ask yourself empowering questions and you will be amazed at how quickly you develop positive habits that guarantee a good, if not great, day every day. Situations will dictate the right questions to ask yourself.

There are twenty empowering questions that I ask myself on a regular basis. Without a doubt, they put magic in my life. Be aware that the empowering questions you create and use do not have to be lengthy and profound – simplicity is often most effective. Discover the magic in asking the right questions as you apply some of these questions in your life.

MY FAVORITE 20 QUESTIONS

1. *How can I make it **fun**?*
2. *What is **great** about this?*
3. *What am I **thankful** for?*
4. *What's a **better way** of looking at this?*
5. *What is my **desired outcome**?*
6. *What is a **possible solution**?*
7. *What did I **learn** from this?*
8. *How can I **simplify** this?*
9. *What would a **Power Thinker** do in this situation?*
10. *What's the **best use** of my time right now?*

11. What **action** do I need to take?

12. **Why** do I want to do this?

13. What are the **benefits**?

14. How can I **feel better** right now?

15. How can I raise my **energy** level?

16. What do I want to **accomplish** today?

17. How can I be more **productive**?

18. What do I **value** most in my life?

19. What's a better choice to **focus** on?

20. What's a **more empowering** question to ask?

 One of the most effective ways to form an empowering question is to establish your desired outcome and then create your question.

You can use some of these 20 empowering questions and substitute your desired outcome in a fill-in-the-blank capacity. For example, with questions 1, 2, and 17, you could *substitute the following:*

1. How can I make it *fun?*
   challenging?
   interesting?
   exciting?
   profitable?

2. What is *great* about this?
   humorous
   inspiring
   special
   unique

17. How can I be more *productive?*
                                energetic?
                                compassionate?
                                intelligent?
                                successful?

Use your imagination and have fun creating your personal empowering questions.

△ *Questions direct focus. Focus determines feelings.*

△ *There are two types of questions that elicit an emotional response: Disempowering Questions (DQs) and Empowering Questions (EQs).*

△ *The "right questions" are the empowering ones.*

△ *For your desired outcome – ask, answer, act, acknowledge, and adjust.*

△ *The quality of your life is determined by the quality of your questions. Do you desire a better life? Ask better questions.*

Manage Your Emotions: Rate Your State

*Every negative emotion
has a disempowering question
holding it in place.*

BILL MAYER

STOP THE INSANITY!

Some people's lives are like a roller coaster ride. Their emotions go up and down, up and down, up and down. Considering all the challenges of life, this is understandable. The key to positive life transformation – that is, a happier, healthier life – is to stabilize your emotional roller coaster ride by keeping the ups and neutral zones far greater than the downs. As a Power Thinker, one of your greatest strengths will be that your positive emotions will significantly outnumber your negative emotions.

How do you stop the insanity of a crazy, up-and-down emotional roller coaster ride? Ask yourself the right questions – the empowering ones.

NEGATIVE EMOTIONAL IMPRISONMENT

To be a positive, mentally healthy, functioning human being, you must reduce the negative emotional lows in your life.

 I believe that every negative emotion has a disempowering question holding it in place.

Harold was married to Thelma for fifteen years. Harold decided to leave Thelma for his much younger personal secretary, Angela. Thelma was extremely angry. She kept asking herself over and over again two disempowering questions: "How could he do this to me?" and "Why is this happening to me?" With questions like this, she found many reasons to support her anger. With each reason (answer), she reinforced and locked in the negative emotion that was causing her pain and upset.

You don't have to discover the exact questions that are holding your negative emotion in place. But understand that you are perpetuating your negative emotion by continually asking and answering the same disempowering questions over and over again. **If you think angry or depressed thoughts, you are asking yourself angry or depressed triggering questions.** The solution is to replace the angry or depressed disempowering questions with empowering questions.

Learning about the principles of Power Thinking and wanting to break out from her negative emotional imprisonment, Thelma began asking herself positive empowering questions. "What specific action can I take right now to feel calmer, more in control, and better about myself?" She followed that with another empowering question, "Knowing that Harold might never return, how can I best get on with my life?"

The answers to these questions will definitely put her in a healthier emotional state. Refer to the following illustration to observe how Thelma's emotional roller coaster ride was stabilized once she started asking herself empowering questions. I'm not saying this is easy, but if you force yourself to create, ask, and then answer your empowering questions, you will enable yourself to feel better. Your alternative is to stay stuck in your negative emotion and be miserable. You do have a choice!

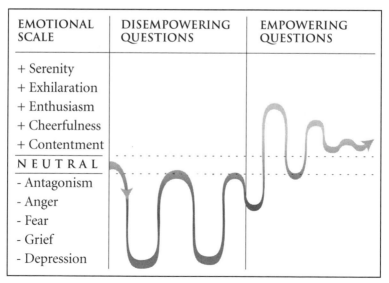

EMOTIONAL SCALE	DISEMPOWERING QUESTIONS	EMPOWERING QUESTIONS
+ Serenity		
+ Exhilaration		
+ Enthusiasm		
+ Cheerfulness		
+ Contentment		
NEUTRAL		
- Antagonism		
- Anger		
- Fear		
- Grief		
- Depression		

THELMA'S EMOTIONAL RESPONSE

YOU HAVE A CHOICE!

I don't believe that all negative emotions can be eliminated, but they can certainly be reduced. By understanding that negative emotions are held in place by disempowering questions, you can spend *less* time experiencing negative emotions. When angry, for example, you can lighten up and take control of the situation by asking, "How long do I *choose* to be angry or hateful or depressed?" Five minutes? Five days? Five months? Five years? There are people who choose to stay angry for years – even a lifetime! It may sound simplistic, but the fact is, **you do have a choice**. As a Power Thinker, be a smarter manager of your emotional states. If you are experiencing a negative emotion, *choose* to stay "stuck in it" for a short period of time.

As you have seen, asking empowering questions is an effective way to help manage and guide your emotions in a positive direction. It is perfectly okay to acknowledge that you are experiencing a negative emotion. "Yes, I'm angry!" But then take charge to reverse your negative emotional state. Declare, "I choose not to remain angry!" Then ask yourself an empowering question, "What's a better way to view this situation?" Use your creativity to come up with a specific empowering question that is appropriate to move you *away* from the negative emotion you are experiencing.

RATE YOUR STATE

You don't have to wait until you experience a negative emotion to implement any of the Power Thinker's emotional-state management techniques that have been discussed. You can take charge – responsibly and consciously managing your emotions – by monitoring them at least once an hour. If you sincerely want to master your emotions, invest in a watch with an alarm. During your *awake hours*, set it to go off once every hour. When you hear the alarm, ask yourself, "How do I feel?" Take time to "rate your state."

Use the following scale of one to ten to **Rate Your State.**

I FEEL. . .

10 ——▸ *Better than Excellent*

9 ——▸ *Excellent*

8 ——▸ *Very Good*

7 ——▸ *Good*

6 ——▸ *Better than O.K.*

5 ——▸ *O.K.*

4 ——▸ *Less than O.K.*

3 ——▸ *Bad*

2 ——▸ *Very Bad*

1 ——▸ *Depressed*

The Rate Your State Scale was intentionally meant to be simplistic. It was not designed to be overly scientific or psychologically analytical. It was designed simply to get in touch with how you generally feel at different moments throughout the day. By being aware of your overall emotional state and energy level, you have a better opportunity to improve your condition. If you're happy with your score after you "rate your state," fantastic! If you're not where you want to be – say you're at a three or four level – simply ask yourself an empowering question, "What can I do to feel better, to feel happier, or to feel more energetic?"

Personalize your empowering question toward your desired emotional state. Ask yourself, "How would I like to feel?" Follow your response to this question with, "What do I have to do to feel this way?" Challenge yourself to see if within a month's time you can consistently keep your emotional state at a "seven" or above.

Awareness is powerful if you use it and then apply the magic in asking the right questions.

Δ *Negative emotions are held in place by disempowering questions.*

Δ *Ask better questions. Replace disempowering questions with empowering ones.*

Δ *Choose to spend less time stuck in negative emotions and more time experiencing positive emotions.*

Δ *Monitor your emotions: Rate your state.*

Morning and Evening Power-Thinking Questions

We always have time enough,
if we will but use it aright.

JOHANN WOLFGANG VON GOETHE

MORNING MAGIC

When? – The first thirty minutes of your day. Do you truly want to take control of your life and create your ultimate dream destiny? Then take full unequivocal control of your conscious thoughts the very second you wake up in the morning. How? With Morning Power-Thinking Questions.

Start your day off with a series of morning questions that are guaranteed to wake you up with an **attitude of gratitude, love, happiness, purpose, and a zest and enthusiasm for life.** While lying comfortably in bed, spend the first ten minutes of your awake time answering specific questions. You can add to and personalize these, of course. I recommend the following five wake-up questions.

MORNING
POWER-THINKING QUESTIONS

1. *What am I **thankful** for?*
2. *Whom do I **love** and who loves me?*
3. *What am I **happy** about ?*
4. *What gives me a **sense of purpose**?*
5. *What am I **excited** and **passionate** about?*

The goal of these questions is to elicit positive emotions that induce a feeling of well-being. After you answer each specific question, ask yourself, "How does that make me feel?" This helps to recognize and reinforce your positive emotions. You'll be amazed how your overall attitude for the day will dramatically improve.

Sam woke up a little depressed and was "fighting" these morning questions. Sam said, "I'm not thankful for or happy about anything in my life right now."

I suggested he insert the word "could" into his questions. He said, "What?" I explained, "What *could* you be thankful for in your life? What *could* you be happy about in your life?" He still fought it some more, then sheepishly responded, "I guess I'm thankful I have a roof over my head. I'm thankful I have good friends. I'm happy that I get to run on the beach every day. I'm happy that I'm going on vacation next week." Sam smiled at me and added, "I guess life is not so bad after all." His morning started to look a little brighter.

AFFIRMATIONS

The middle ten minutes of Morning Magic should be devoted to affirmations – **positive self-talk.** Your subconscious mind is most impressionable and openly receptive to new information from the conscious mind immediately after you wake up in the morning. It's like a sponge soaking up new data that can override past negative habitual thinking patterns. You can repeat these affirmations while in the shower or washing your face at the sink or whenever it's most convenient for you.

Affirmations on their own are effective. Affirmations repeated with strong emotions and exaggerated physiology, such as clapping your hands or clenching your fist, are more effective. Affirmations followed by a positive empowering question are most effective. For example, after ten repetitions of "I am responsible," then ask yourself, "What are the personal benefits of being responsible?" By asking and answering your empowering question, you strengthen your belief and conviction which compels you to take action.

What affirmations would be best for you to use? Make up an ongoing **Be-Do-Have** list of at least ten items each of how you want to be, what you want to do, and what you want to have. This is your goals list. Simply ask yourself, "How do I really want to be? What would I love to do? What would give me tremendous pleasure to have?" Refer to the following illustration for an example of a Be-Do-Have goals list.

BE	DO	HAVE
Energetic	Professional Speaking	Big-Screen TV
Cheerful	Speed Reading	Jaguar XJ6
Honest	Learn Spanish	New Running Shoes
Confident	Take Memory Course	One Massage/Week
Healthy	Australian Vacation	Credit Cards Paid Off
Neat	One New Word/Day	Compact Disk Player
Creative	Dental Checkup	Ocean View Home
Intelligent	Morning Questions	$100,000 in Savings
Focused	Write a Book	Golden Lab Retriever
Spiritual	Workout 6 Times/Week	New Wardrobe

BE-DO-HAVE GOALS LIST

If you want to improve who you are, take a few moments right now and put together your personal Be-Do-Have goals list.

From this list, form one "Be," one "Do," and one "Have" affirmation and use these three affirmations as the middle ten minutes of your Morning Magic for at least one week. Sunday night is an ideal time to prepare the following week's affirmations. Keep affirmations personal and positive toward your desired outcome by using "I." Keep them in present time as if they were being accomplished – "I am" or "I have" for example. Remember, to make affirmations more believable and powerful, always follow them with an empowering question.

"Be" Affirmation – "I am enthusiastic and passionate about life!" After ten repetitions, follow with the question, "How could I live my life with more enthusiasm and passion?"

"Do" Affirmation – "I learn one new vocabulary word each day." Follow with the question, "How does this benefit me?"

"Have" Affirmation – "I own a forty-five-inch big-screen television." Follow with the question, "What pleasure will I derive from having this?"

An effective technique that you can use when you create your affirmations is to place three words – *I choose to* – in front of whatever you want to be, do, or have. Follow with the question *Why?* If you were to apply this technique to the preceding affirmations, they would read as follows:

> 1. *I choose to be enthusiastic and passionate about life.*
> 2. *I choose to learn one new vocabulary word each day.*
> 3. *I choose to own a forty-five-inch big-screen television.*

Using the expression "I choose to" implies that you are taking responsibility for, and have the power to create, your desired to be, to do, or to have outcomes. Asking *why* provides reasons and thus strengthens your belief in your affirmation and encourages a call to action.

Whatever technique you use, spend approximately ten minutes on affirmations. With each one of the three Be-Do-Have types, allocate about one minute for ten repetitions of the affirmation, one minute for answering the empowering question that follows the affirmation, and one minute for visualizing your desired outcome of the affirmation. There is tremendous power in visualization! If you trust that what you vividly see in your mind's eye is your reality having already happened, then whatever you dream to be, to do, or to have will soon be yours.

I was approached by a friend recently who commented, "I like the concept of the Be-Do-Have list, but having ten items under each goal category is overwhelming to me. How can I simplify this?" I told him to set up three **Power-Thinking Triangles**. By starting with one Be, one Do, and one Have triangle, you can form basic affirmations. At the top of each triangle, write down your most important Be, Do, or Have goal. Use these to put together your first three morning affirmations. The bottom two corners at the base of each triangle can be your "on deck" goals for future affirmations. For example:

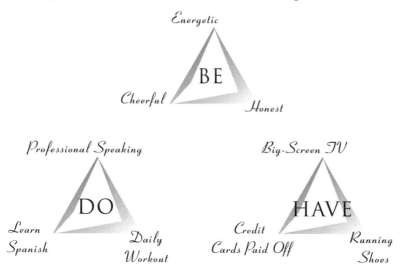

Using the above Power-Thinking Triangles, your first week's affirmations would be formed from the goal at the top of each triangle:

Δ To **be** energetic

Δ To **do** professional speaking

Δ To **have** a big-screen TV

At the appropriate time you can change to a new affirmation simply by rotating, in a clockwise direction, to get a new Be, Do, or Have goal. *Appropriate time* should be a minimum of one week and a maximum of one month. If, in the immediate future, you want to continue to work on the goal that was on the top of the triangle, then move it to the bottom right corner (the second "on deck" position). For example:

If you're happy with your affirmation results regarding the goal at the top of the triangle, check it off indicating that it has been accomplished. Then do your normal clockwise rotation and fill in the vacant bottom right-hand corner with a new goal. For example:

Once you choose to focus on a particular goal at some level of awareness, you will always be working on that goal. The Be-Do-Have Power-Thinking Triangles were designed to make it easier for you to focus on one goal at a time.

Use the last ten minutes of your Morning Magic to plan your day. You can do this as part of a morning walk or while sitting down at your breakfast table – whatever works for you. Ask, "What do I want to accomplish today?" Keep it simple. Make a list. Prioritize it and then take action by doing one thing at a time. Don't simply go through the motions of life. Enjoy your day! As you're checking off your list, continually ask yourself, in reference to that day's activities, "How can I make it fun?" I refer to my daily list of things to do as my "Feel Good List." Whenever I complete doing something on this list and check it off, I expect to feel good! A sample list looks like this:

Apply Morning Magic	☺✓
Meditate – A.M. & P.M.	☺
Learn Word for the Day	☺✓
Workout Gym/Run Beach	☺✓
Drink 64 Ounces H$_2$O	☺
Teach Tennis Lessons	☺✓
Listen to Memory Tapes	☺✓
Pay Credit-Card Bills	☺✓
Plan Australian Vacation	☺
Read for Personal Growth	☺✓

FEEL GOOD LIST

So there you have it, Morning Magic – your thirty magical morning minutes:

*Ten minutes for **Morning Questions***

*Ten minutes for **Affirmations***

*Ten minutes for **Planning your Day***

Of course, if you want to spend more time in any specific category, go for it!

EVENING MAGIC

What's another time of day that you might want to take advantage of your subconscious mind's open-door policy? Right before you go to sleep at night. Apply these bedtime questions.

EVENING
        POWER-THINKING QUESTIONS

1. *What did I learn today?*

2. *How did I contribute to others today?*

3. *Was today a personal growth day? Am I a better person today than I was yesterday?*

4. *Am I moving toward my major definite purpose?*

5. *What are three things that are important for me to accomplish tomorrow? (This gives the subconscious mind time to work on these three while you sleep.)*

You might consider keeping a daily journal. Many successful individuals have developed the habit of recording their thoughts for the day in a personal growth journal. If your life is worth living, then certainly it is worth recording. Even taking just five minutes will be time well-invested in yourself.

It is always comforting to go to sleep with loving and appreciative thoughts. The two following morning questions are perfect questions to repeat as your last thoughts of the day: "Whom do I love and who loves me?" and "What am I thankful for?"

Good night, sleep tight, and plant the seeds of thought that will make your life right.

Δ The "rudder of your day" is your thirty
minutes of Morning Magic.

Δ Ask yourself morning questions of thanks,
love, happiness, purpose, and zest.

Δ Affirm your Be-Do-Have goals. Support
your beliefs with empowering questions.

Δ Plan your day: List, prioritize, and act.

Δ Ask yourself evening questions to check
your personal growth and to plant
seeds for your subconscious mind.

$\mathcal{LTQ}$: *Learning Through Questions*

He who asks questions
cannot avoid the answers.

ANCIENT PROVERB

QUESTIONS ARE THE ANSWER

Questions are the primary and most effective way to learn practically anything. Who was the first president of the United States? How do you spell Mississippi? This power of learning through questions started in ancient Greece with the philosopher Socrates. The Socratic Method basically directed the student's focus through questions, allowing him to formulate his own answers. It is not my intent to expound on the Socratic Method. You can do that by simply going to your local library. Instead, I want you to understand that as a Power Thinker, you can dramatically enhance your learning skills, expand your knowledge, and improve your life by asking yourself learning-directed and growth-oriented questions on a daily basis.

Tony had a passion for learning. He prided himself on using questions as a personal growth tool. He would regularly ask himself questions like, "What book can I read? What tape can I listen to? What seminar can I attend that will help propel me into the top five percent in my present profession?" Whenever he completed a job or task, he would ask himself, "What did I learn from this? What would I continue to do? What could I improve on?" Like Tony, learn and grow by relentlessly asking yourself empowering questions.

PERSONAL GROWTH POWER PAD

One of the very best investments that you will ever make in yourself and your future is a yellow legal-size writing pad. Make this your personal growth power pad. I refer to mine as my Q&A Power-Thinking Pad. At the top of the pad, write "Question for the Day." A good question to start off with – one that I recently asked myself – is, "What would I like to learn that will help me on my personal growth journey?" I responded, "I'd like to learn speed-reading, a new language, computers and the Internet, the basics of investing money, and how to meditate."

Challenge yourself and your creativity to come up with at least ten answers to your *question for the day*. Make a list and prioritize it. Ask an empowering question specific to each new idea on this list and then take action on your responses. For example: "What's the best way for me to get started on learning to speed-read?" Your response and call to action might be, "I will sign up for an Evelyn Wood speed-reading course starting next Monday."

Questions for the day regarding learning are highly effective in helping you on your personal growth journey. You can also ask empowering questions regarding anything that is presently going on in your life that you would like to focus on, for example, your goals list. How do you want to be? Where would you love to travel? What would you like to own? The simple act of taking time, on a daily basis, to write down questions regarding your desires – where you want to go with your life, and what you would like to learn – will put you in an elite minority of individuals who are truly trying to consciously improve themselves and their lives. Learning through questions is growing through questions!

As a parent, a great question to ask your child is, "What did you learn today?"

ARE YOU CHEATING YOURSELF?

Do you have goals, dreams, hopes, and aspirations? If so, it is your responsibility to consistently ask yourself two questions, "Where do I want to go?" and "How do I want to grow?" Understand that if you continually ask yourself questions that take you *away* from where you want to go and grow, or if you neglect to ask questions that will take you *toward* where you want to go and grow, you're cheating yourself.

Take advantage of the magic in asking the right questions, and apply the empowering question-asking techniques you have learned thus far to the thirteen types of Power Thinking which are described in the next chapter.

Δ *Questions are the answer.*

Δ *Your Q&A Power-Thinking Pad stimulates personal growth through questions and answers.*

Δ *Parent to child, "What did you learn today?"*

Δ *Ask yourself, "Where do I want to go? How do I want to grow?"*

CHAPTER 3

Power-Thinking Types: A Baker's Dozen

The greatest power a person possesses
is the power to choose.

J. MARTIN KOHE

13 UNIQUE WAYS TO THINK

First, let's define Power Thinking.

Power Thinking is consistently asking yourself
empowering questions, to control your conscious
thoughts, to create the destiny you desire.

Because of the significance of this definition, I am breaking it down into its three major components and clarifying each one. Power Thinking is

1. *Consistently asking yourself empowering questions.*
   Continually ask yourself questions that, when
   answered and acted on, will stimulate positive

emotions and put you in a better state of mind. They are questions that will strengthen you.

2. *Control your conscious thoughts. Direct your present-time thoughts.*

3. *Create the destiny you desire. Create the desired outcomes in your life of how you want to be and feel, and what you want to do and have.*

I have created thirteen Power Thinking categories, or types. Each one has life-transforming potential, and all have been helpful to me on my personal growth journey.

Remember that this knowledge, as with all knowledge, is powerful only when applied. Happy reading and happy applying!

13 TYPES OF POWER THINKING

Directional

Purposeful

Present-Time

Habitual

Focused

Happy

Creative

Self-Esteem

Positive

Responsible

Healthy

Prosperity

Simplified

Directional Power Thinking

*If you don't know where you want to go,
any road will take you there.*

CHESHIRE CAT, ALICE IN WONDERLAND

BUMPER CAR MENTALITY

Too often in life, people react to external circumstances and events, bouncing around and wandering aimlessly with no sense of direction. Their lives sometimes appear to be one big accident, seemingly out of control.

What's the solution to this haphazard lifestyle? Decide to use your mind as your "master guide," as it is the most powerful *compass* ever created. Your life can be guided only by where your mind directs you. You can control your mind and thoughts, and therefore control the direction and results in your life. Zig Ziglar, motivational speaker, wisely advises, "Don't be a wandering generality; be a meaningful specific."

Because you reap what you sow in your *mind's garden*, you must carefully select the goals and game plans you *plant* for your life. Specific goals will give you direction, direction will give you a sense of purpose, and a sense of purpose will give you a feeling of well-being.

Ron was fired from a job where he had been employed for over ten years. He quickly became depressed. His loss of income was a factor, but his *lack of direction* was even more critical. Observing his lethargic and hopeless state, I challenged him to design a game plan for his life. Understanding the magic in empowering questions, I asked him, "What type of work would you *love* to do that you could be *passionate* about?" Ron laughed because he never thought about *designing a life* but only about *making a living*. To him, work was work. You punch in, you do your job, and you punch out. The concept of doing what you love to do was foreign, yet intriguing to him. Redirecting his energies to finding a new job that he could be passionate about sparked an enthusiastic fire from within. Fortunately, this burning desire propelled him out of his depression. Ron's newfound *direction* renewed his sense of purpose and restored a feeling of excitement and well-being about his life.

CLICHÉS

Clichés evolve over the years because there appears to be a consistent truth about them. One such goal-related cliché is, "Failing to plan is planning to fail." Simple, clear, precise, and true. Lack of knowledge about the power of goals causes many individuals to *fail to plan*. For some people, goals can be intimidating to initiate because of their numerous classifications – spiritual, emotional, financial, mental, social, family, and so forth. For others, sitting down to plan their future by writing down all of these diverse categories is overwhelming and burdensome.

To ensure that they do not *fail to plan,* Directional Power Thinkers simplify their goals. They make their goals easier by listing them in three distinct categories – Be, Do, and Have. "How would you like to *be*?" Perhaps more energetic. "What do you want to *do*?" Perhaps travel to Australia. "What do you desire to *have*?" Perhaps a new car. To give yourself specific direction in your life, it is beneficial to have at least three Be, three Do, and three Have goals at all times.

Goals also have the negative stigma attached to them of being boring. "Oh no! Not goals again!" But only boring goals are boring. I overcame this negativism by referring to each one of my goals as a DWAG – a Dream With A Game plan. Instantaneously my goals became more interesting and exciting. Dreams tend to inspire us, and having a game plan implies two things: The goals will be written down and action will be taken on them.

 Until a goal is written down, it is simply a wish.

Do you sometimes experience life with a "bumper car" mentality? Is life controlling you rather than you controlling your life? If so, then choose to live your life with a more responsible, goal-oriented mental approach, and apply Directional Power Thinking.

How do you initiate Directional Power Thinking? With **Directional Power-Thinking questions.** Check out the following examples:

- *What type of work would I love to do that I could feel passionate about?*
- *What are the most significant goals in my life right now?*
- *Where would I most enjoy vacationing anywhere in the world?*
- *What would I dare to dream to do if I knew I could not fail?*
- *When I die – referring to accomplishments and virtues – how would I like my epitaph to read?*

Upon reviewing these questions and this chapter, the Cheshire Cat had a change of heart. He was overheard saying, "If you do know where you want to go, then specific roads will take you there." Directional Power Thinkers have a definite game plan for their lives.

Create and answer one or more of your own Directional Power-Thinking questions. It's imperative to take the time and effort to formulate and then answer at least one empowering question, specific to your needs, at the end of each Power-Thinking section. It will individualize and, as a result, speed up your personal growth journey. Know that the terms *Power-Thinking questions* and *empowering questions* are synonymous and can be used interchangeably.

When you are personalizing your question for each one of the thirteen types of Power Thinking, be certain to do some cerebral searching. Your mind is like a gold mine – full of treasures. Your challenge is to learn to "mine your mind" for golden insights. Do you really want to improve yourself? No one ever said thinking was easy, but it is rewarding.

Create and answer your own Directional Power-Thinking question.

△ *Your mind is the powerful compass that directs your life.*

△ *Failing to plan is planning to fail.*

△ *Three types of goals are Be, Do, and Have.*

△ *A DWAG is a Dream With A Game plan.*

△ *Mine your mind.*

Purposeful Power Thinking

Above all have a single aim;
have a legitimate and useful purpose and
devote yourself unreservedly to it.

JAMES ALLEN

RAISON D'ÊTRE

The English translation of *raison d'être* is "reason to be." Have you ever asked yourself why you were born on this planet Earth? To live? To learn? To grow? To make a difference? What is your reason to be? Your response does not have to be profound. You don't have to cure cancer or be a rocket scientist. Being the most loving, caring, and supportive parent is a fantastic reason to be. A school teacher, sanitation engineer, doctor, or mechanic committed to being the best – in whichever chosen field – is also exceptional.

A sense of purpose creates positive energy. I've never met a depressed person who had clearly defined goals and a sense of purpose. Power Thinkers recognize that purpose is more significant than outcome. Who you become, while in the *process*, is more important than the results you create or the actual achievement of a specific goal. Sense of purpose ignites an ongoing personal growth process that stimulates vitality, enthusiasm, and a passion for life.

WHY ASK WHY?

Purposeful Power Thinkers acknowledge that desire is a great motivator. When establishing and writing down their goals, they always ask *why* – "Why do I want to achieve this specific goal?" Because the more *reasons* and *benefits* you have for the attainment of a goal, the more desire and conviction you have to take action and go for it! If reasons *why* are established, then emotions are intensified, beliefs are strengthened, and goals are more rapidly achieved.

Power Thinkers challenge their sense of purpose when they ask the following "Three-D" questions:

1. **Direction** – *Where do I want to go with my life?*
2. **Desire** – *How badly do I want it and why?*
3. **Dedication** – *How disciplined am I? Do I have a single-minded focus of concentration to go for it?*

Doing what they love to do and providing extraordinary service to others are trademarks of Power Thinkers who successfully fulfill their sense of purpose. Find your purpose, commit and dedicate yourself to that purpose, focus unwaveringly on it, and strive for excellence! The ultimate rewards of your character development and improved self-esteem will be invaluable.

Now let's jump-start Purposeful Power Thinking. How? Through **Purposeful Power-Thinking questions.** Here are some examples:

- *What cause can I become actively involved in to make a meaningful difference? (You might, for example, become involved with the Special Olympics, Big Brothers, or Literacy Volunteers.)*
- *What do I value most in my life right now? (Your sense of purpose should be in harmony with your values.)*
- *With my unique skills, what beneficial service can I provide to positively affect the lives of hundreds of people?*
- *What specific classes can I take, books can I read, or seminars can I attend to improve my communication skills as a parent, spouse, boyfriend, or girlfriend?*
- *What do I do that gives me the greatest feeling of importance, mental well-being, and self-worth?*

Your sense of purpose, specifically your *major definite purpose* in life, is often triggered by answering this last question. It is a key indicator of your area of excellence, and the hallmark of integrity in life is doing what you love to do.

Use your creative imagination to come up with at least one Purposeful Power-Thinking question appropriate for you. Then take the time to answer it – you're worth it!

Create and answer your own Purposeful Power-Thinking question.

In closing, here is a brief poem I recently composed:

RAISON D'ÊTRE

Who are you?
Why are you here?
What are you committed to?
What do you fear?

Open your eyes,
And you shall see,
With the magic in questions,
Your reason to be!

Δ Raison d'être means reason to be.

Δ Purpose is more significant than outcome.

Δ Apply the power of asking Why?
Reasons intensify emotions and action.

Δ The "Three-D" sense-of-purpose
questions help you define direction,
desire, and dedication.

Present-Time Power Thinking

*I know of no more encouraging fact than the
unquestionable ability of man to elevate
his life by a conscious endeavor.*

HENRY DAVID THOREAU

NOWISM

Nowism is a term I created that means living in the *now*, the moment. Nowism is living **consciously** – simply put, it is **present-time awareness.**

The contrary is living unconsciously. Unconscious thoughts are thoughts of the past that are stored in your "mind's library," the subconscious mind. This library comprises every thought and belief you've ever had, and, whether real or imagined, the subconscious mind has accepted the incoming information to be true. Subconscious means *below the conscious awareness level.* To better understand nowism and its importance, study the following illustration.

*S*TATES OF AWARENESS
"NOWISM"

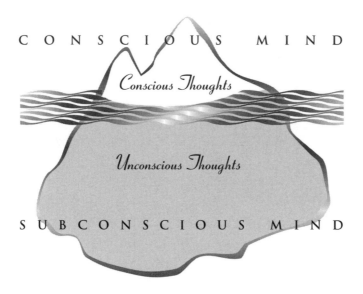

C O N S C I O U S   M I N D

Conscious Thoughts

Unconscious Thoughts

S U B C O N S C I O U S   M I N D

Think of your conscious thoughts as the tip of the iceberg and your unconscious thoughts as the much larger base and body of the iceberg. We are all a mold of our countless past thoughts, beliefs, and experiences. Consequently, the majority of our thoughts are of an unconscious nature. Which do you think are more powerful? Unfortunately, it's the *unconscious thoughts* in the *subconscious mind*. Simply look at the difference in the size of them!

REACTIVE VERSUS PROACTIVE

You don't have control of your subconscious mind. It **reacts**, responding on automatic pilot, in a stimulus-response mode, to the information it receives. The stimuli are your incoming thoughts. The response is a robot-like sorting process by your subconscious mind. It instantaneously compares your incoming thoughts with similar past thoughts and responds automatically, based on this information.

On the contrary, **you can control your conscious mind.** Where your subconscious mind is *reactive* and deals with past thoughts, your conscious mind is *proactive* and deals with present thoughts. Proactive implies you're in the driver's seat of your thought mobile – you're in control.

BOMBARDING TECHNIQUE

Even though you can't control your subconscious mind, you can control the conscious thoughts that go into your subconscious mind. With your present-time awareness, be sure to continually fill your subconscious mind with positive thoughts. You do this by "bombarding" your subconscious mind with positive present-time empowering conscious thoughts on a daily basis. **This process will increase your ratio of positive to negative thoughts in your subconscious mind.** The following illustration clarifies this.

BOMBARD YOUR SUBCONSCIOUS MIND
with
POSITIVE, CONSCIOUS THOUGHTS, AND...

move from this to this

C O N S C I O U S   M I N D

Unconscious Thoughts
75% NEGATIVE
25% POSITIVE

Unconscious Thoughts
25% NEGATIVE
75% POSITIVE

S U B C O N S C I O U S   M I N D

IMPROVING STATES OF AWARENESS

These percentages are simply hypothetical numbers. The subconscious mind typically has a higher percentage of negative unconscious thoughts before the bombarding technique is applied.

The end result – after being bombarded – is that when your subconscious mind responds *automatically*, it will do so in a more positive fashion. Why is this so important? Because of the awesome power of the subconscious mind.

Be more aware of your conscious thoughts, because every thought you ever have will be recorded and stored in your subconscious mind. This mental library will affect your emotional states and your well-being for the rest of your life. By applying this bombarding technique, your ratio of positive to negative thoughts within your subconscious mind will steadily increase. As a result, the overall quality of your thoughts and quality of your life will significantly improve.

ADDITIONAL PRESENT-TIME BENEFITS

Long-range personal growth is an inevitable outcome of applying this bombarding technique as a lifetime process. There are other, more immediate, benefits of being a Present-Time Power Thinker. You will instantly reap the rewards of positive conscious thoughts with a positive feeling. If you think happy present-time thoughts, you will experience a feeling of happiness in the moment.

You can also use present-time empowering questions to tap into and access your positive unconscious thoughts in your subconscious mind. The amazing benefit of developing this skill is that you can be 90% negative and only 10% positive in a particular area of your life, yet the empowering question can access the 10% positive.

Richard dreaded giving speeches. I asked him, "What do you think about public speaking?" He responded, "I hate it!" He was simply responding on automatic pilot. Ninety percent of his unconscious thoughts in his subconscious mind were negative about public speaking. Sorting through his past experiences, his little "robot" reminded him of three things – he got nervous in front of groups, he often forgot his speeches, and he once tripped while walking up to the podium.

When I first asked Richard the empowering question, "What's great about public speaking?" his response was, "Absolutely nothing!" I asked the same question again and added, "Was there ever a time that you felt good about speaking?" This helped him to access his 10% positive past thoughts and experiences regarding speaking. He said, "Once I gave a speech and I really felt *in power.* Another time I had the feeling I was really *making a difference* in somebody's life. It felt great!"

Just moments ago he said he hated speaking. Are you beginning to see the value of empowering questions?

Another unique benefit of present-time empowering questions is that it encourages you to create new positive thoughts. I asked Richard one last question, "What *could* be great about public speaking?" He thought about it for a minute and then replied. "With practice, maybe I could overcome my fear of speaking – that would be a big win for me. With some success, I would be more confident, which would really help my self-esteem." He came up with three more reasons about what could be great about public speaking. With each one he got a little more excited. With his newfound enthusiasm, Richard said he was going to join Toastmasters and challenge himself to be a better speaker. There truly is power in empowering questions!

 You can't control your past – but you can create your future!

As a Present-Time Power Thinker, controlling your *conscious* thoughts will be the single most important skill you develop to improve the quality and direction of your life.

Remember:

△ *Your thoughts control your life and destiny.*

△ *You can control your conscious thoughts.*

△ *You can control your destiny!*

This central theme has been and will be repeated over and over, since it is a core belief of Power Thinking. To become the creator, sculptor, and architect of your destiny, you must develop and master the fundamental skill of gaining control of your conscious thoughts through the magic in asking the right questions.

Empowering questions are effective because they can change your awareness state from negative and unconscious to positive and conscious. Present time – in the moment – now – is where you want to live your life.

Here are some examples of **Present-Time Power-Thinking questions:**

- *What can I do right now to raise my energy level?*
- *How can I make today a special day?*
- *What's beautiful in my immediate environment?*
- *What's great about this situation?*
- *How can I make it fun? (This is a great question to ask before doing any chore or activity.)*

Create and answer your own Present-Time Power-Thinking question.

In closing, enjoy reading this wonderfully insightful poem, a view of life from a fourteen-year-old boy, Jason Lehman.

PRESENT TENSE

It was spring,
But it was summer I wanted,
The warm days, and the great outdoors.
It was summer,
But it was fall I wanted,
The colorful leaves, and the cool, dry air.
It was fall,
But it was winter I wanted,
The beautiful snow, and the joy of the holiday
    season.
It was winter,
But it was spring I wanted,
The warmth, and the blossoming of nature.
I was a child,
But it was adulthood I wanted,
The freedom, and the respect.
I was twenty,
But it was thirty I wanted,
To be mature, and sophisticated.
I was middle-aged,
But it was twenty I wanted,
The youth, and the free spirit.
I was retired,
But it was middle age I wanted,
The presence of mind, without limitations.
My life was over,
But I never got what I wanted.

What a tragedy to waste life away in the past, the future, or some other time. Had the person in this poem applied Present-Time Power-Thinking skills, he might have realized that he had much, or perhaps all, of what he wanted.

Δ *Nowism is present-time awareness.*

Δ *Bombard your subconscious mind with positive conscious thoughts.*

Δ *Control your conscious thoughts by asking yourself empowering questions.*

Habitual Power Thinking

*We first make our habits and
then our habits make us.*

JOHN DRYDEN

HABITOLOGY

Habitology is the science of the cause-and-effect
relationship between thoughts and habits. Thoughts
stimulate action and, regularly repeated, actions form
habits. Habits are the foundation of a person's character. "We
are what we repeatedly do," observed Aristotle.

Habitual Power Thinking is consistently choosing to use
positive empowering thoughts to develop habits that will help
build your character and shape your destiny. It's combining
positive conscious thoughts with *self-discipline* – the key
ingredient for developing good habits. Because habits are

manifestations of thoughts, and thoughts are initiated by questions, a simplified Character Building Cycle would look like the following illustration.

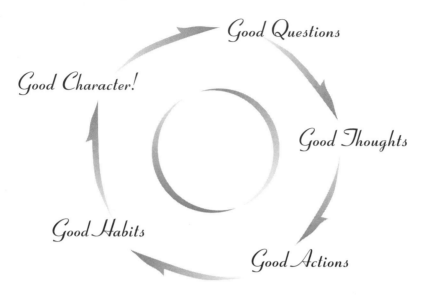

CHARACTER BUILDING CYCLE

Self-discipline is the *mental training* that develops your *self-control*. It is the glue that bonds this Character Building Cycle together. Self-discipline is exemplified by your dedication, commitment, and persistence, which ultimately reinforces your good habits through repetition.

The cause (thought) and effect (habit) nature of habitology is summarized wisely by the past president of the New York Bar Association, Orison Swett Marden. He observes, "The beginning of a habit is like an invisible thread, but every time we repeat the act we strengthen the strand, add to it another filament, until it becomes a great cable and binds us irrevocably, thought and act."

You can break bad habits with the help of Habitual Power-Thinking questions.

The first step in breaking a bad habit is to acknowledge that you have one. The first question you should ask yourself if you want to break a bad habit is "**Why?**" A simple, yet very empowering question. "Why do I want to break the bad habit?" Your reasons why will give you strength and conviction to take action.

Typically, your reasons *why* are related to things that you *value.* Jim decided he wanted to stop smoking. The following are two of his ten responses as to why he wanted to stop smoking. He wanted to "breathe easier so that he could work out more regularly" – he valued his health. He wanted to "live longer so he could see his newborn son grow up" – he valued his family.

Jim then decided to use these personal answers to create Habitual Power-Thinking questions relating to these values. Whenever he felt the desire to light up a cigarette, Jim would ask himself two questions. One, "Is this something a healthy person would do?" and two, "Is this something a dad who wants to see his son grow up would do?" The answer to both questions was a resounding "No!" Two weeks later Jim stopped smoking completely, and he hasn't lit up since. The more reasons you have for breaking a bad habit, the more conviction you will have in taking action to do so.

Good habits are usually developed in areas of your life that are important to you – things that you value. Jennifer valued neatness – her office was always tidy. Kurt valued promptness – he was always on time. Some good habits are seemingly inborn, almost natural. Others need to be developed.

The best way to develop good habits is to first establish a *desired outcome,* something worthy of developing good habits for. This is done by asking yourself, "How do I want to be?" or "What do I want to do?" or "What do I want to have?"

Being skinny all his life, Dan was shocked when he got on the scale the other day. It read 199, almost 200 pounds. Wow! The answer to his question, "How do I want to be?" came very quickly to him. "I want to be in shape, muscularly toned, and 185 pounds!" To get there, he had to develop good habits.

The empowering question Dan asked himself was, "What three habits will best help me reach my desired outcome of 185 pounds?" His response, "Work out regularly, eat healthy, and drink plenty of water."

To get himself to work out regularly, he asked, "How can I make it fun?" Dan made a game out of working out and began to associate more pleasure with exercising. He set up a challenging – yet fun – workout program and actually enjoyed it. Rather than deprive himself of foods he couldn't eat, he made a list of only tasty, healthy foods that he could choose to eat. Although he hasn't stuck with it 100 percent, he's definitely developing the habit of eating fruits and vegetables more regularly. To develop the third habit, Dan wrote down five benefits of drinking more water and made it more readily available by carrying a bottle with him. He went from drinking about a quart of water a day to almost a gallon. Three months later Dan happily proclaimed, "I feel cleansed and energized, and I reached my goal of 185 pounds."

Here are some examples of other **Habitual Power-Thinking questions:**

- *Why do I want to break this bad habit?*
- *What can I do to overcome my negative habit of procrastination?*
- *What are good habits to develop to achieve my goal of _____ ?*
- *What is the best time every day to go for my thirty-minute walk?*
- *What are some wake-up Power-Thinking questions that I can use to jump-start every morning for the next twenty-one days?*

Approximately twenty-one days appears to be the magic number by most "experts" on how long it takes to develop a habit – so stick with it!

Create and answer your own Habitual Power-Thinking question.

Δ *Habits are manifestations of repeated thoughts and actions.*

Δ *Habits are the foundation of a person's character.*

Δ *Good habits are reinforced by strong self-discipline.*

Δ *Develop the habit of asking better, more empowering questions.*

Δ *Empowering questions can help break bad habits and develop good ones.*

Focused Power Thinking

Success. . .

It is focusing the full power of all you are

on what you have a burning desire to achieve.

WILFRED A. PETERSON

HOCUS-POCUS FOCUS

Yes, there also is magic in the power of focus, specifically Focused Power Thinking. How powerful is focus? Every emotional state, positive or negative, is determined by what you focus on – profound and true! What determines what you focus on? Questions – the questions you ask yourself on a daily basis.

Since how you feel is determined by what you focus on, and what you focus on is determined by the questions you ask yourself, then if you want to feel better, **ask yourself better questions!**

Remember the DQs (disempowering questions) and the EQs (empowering questions) we discussed in chapter two? Let me refresh your memory with an example of each one.

DQ example – *"Why is my life so miserable?"*
Your answers are going to **focus on why your life is miserable.** How will this make you feel? Probably depressed.

EQ example – *"How can I make my life better?"*
Your answers will **focus on possible solutions.** How will this make you feel? Maybe not great, but at least okay, with the hope of an improved future – certainly a better emotional state than the DQ put you in.

Common sense tells you that if you increase your empowering questions and decrease your disempowering questions, the quality of your life and overall well-being has to improve. Now that you know this principle, you must be focused, dedicated, and disciplined in applying it. Make a commitment to yourself, starting right now, to consistently ask yourself better, more empowering questions. It will be a decision you will never regret – one that could positively transform your life.

CONCENTRATION

Outside of directly affecting emotional states, Focused Power Thinking also refers to concentration. **Concentration is disciplined focus.** It is described by Komar, a contemporary artist, "Concentration, in its truest, unadulterated form means being able to focus the mind on one solitary thing."

Concentration is the key that opens the door and directs your energy toward achieving your goals and realizing your dreams. The more you continually focus on a specific goal or dream, the more your mental capacities are recruited, dedicated, and applied to making that goal or dream a reality. By concentrating your efforts on a single aim or purpose, your efficiency multiplies. You're more likely to finish what you start, and you're rewarded with an intense feeling of accomplishment.

Thomas A. Edison was once asked, "What's the first requisite for success?" He responded, "The ability to apply your physical and mental energies to one problem incessantly without growing weary. You do something all day long, don't you? Everyone does. If you get up at 7 a.m. and go to bed at 11 p.m., you have put in sixteen good hours, and it is certain with most men that they have been doing something all the time. The only trouble is that they do it about a great many things, and I do it about one. **If they took the time in question and applied it in one direction, to one object, they would succeed.**"

If it works for Mr. Edison, it can also work for you and me. Developing and applying the skill of *disciplined focus* will definitely increase your opportunities for success in your life.

I agree with Thomas Troward's solution for lack of focus or lack of concentration — what he refers to as *scattered thinking*. In his book *The Law and the Word*, he writes, "We are aiming at consciously controlling our mental powers instead of letting them hurry us hither and thither in a purposeless manner."

Remember, as a Power Thinker, you have a choice about what you focus on.

What can help your concentration? **Focused Power-Thinking questions.** Here are some examples:

- *What can I focus on to feel better?*
- *What should I concentrate on to complete this task or goal?*
- *What, on my daily To Do list, do I need to do first?*
- *What's a more empowering choice to focus on?*
- *What's a possible solution? What's a better solution?*

Create and answer your own Focused Power-Thinking question.

Δ *Emotional states are determined by what you focus on.*

Δ *The questions you ask yourself determine your focus.*

Δ *To feel better, ask yourself better questions.*

Δ *Concentration is disciplined, single-minded focus.*

Happy Power Thinking

True happiness
comes from joy of deeds well done,
the zest of creating things new.

ANTOINE DE SAINT-EXUPÉRY

HAPPIOLOGY

Happiology is the science of happiness as defined by Mayer. Happiness is a process – it's working *toward* a worthy goal. It's learning, accomplishing, and achieving. It's utilizing creative and honest efforts toward the fulfillment of your life's purpose. It's the joy of using your full powers toward excellence and living up to your potential. It's problem solving and overcoming obstacles. It's a by-product of *right action* – activities taking you in the direction you choose to go with your life. Happiness is not *attainment and having*, but rather *striving and doing*.

Happiness is the process of personal growth.

Looking for happiness? Live your life as a personal growth journey and happiness will find you! As a Power Thinker, your ultimate happiness is defined as "actively pursuing with passion and progressively realizing your ideal goal."

BEWARE OF HAPPINESS
IF/WHEN RULES

Linda, seemingly distraught and confused, approached me for guidance one day. She said, "I'm really trying to be positive and goal oriented, but I just can't seem to be happy for more than a few fleeting moments – What can I do?" I asked her, "What has to occur for you to be happy?" Without hesitation she replied, "I will be happy **if** I make a minimum of $200,000 per year" and "I will be happy **when** I lose 50 pounds." I inquired, "Do you want to be happy only at the destination of your goal or during the entire journey?" She laughed, saying, "Of course, during the entire journey, or at least most of the time." An *awareness light* went on inside Linda's mind. She was sabotaging herself with her Happiness If/When Rules. She realized that establishing these rigid rules for happiness was setting herself up for failure. If everything didn't go exactly as planned, she was going to be *un*happy.

I reminded Linda that happiness was the process of personal growth. Knowing this, I asked her to reconsider a more empowering response to the question, "What has to occur for you to be happy?" Looking a bit more cheerful, she exclaimed, "I will be happy, no matter how much money I make, as long as I give it my best effort!" She added, "I will be happy losing one pound a week for the next year." She smiled and concluded, "I like this concept of progressively working toward a worthy goal." Because life is always changing, Linda's newfound flexibility and creativity will definitely increase her chances for experiencing happiness more often.

LIGHTEN UP!

An important concept to understand is that the happiest person is the person who is thinking the happiest thoughts. So, if you find yourself taking yourself or life too seriously, then heed this bit of friendly advice – Lighten Up! Heavy thoughts do have *mental mass* and these thoughts can "weigh you down" and make you feel unhappy.

How do you lighten up? Think lighter, happier thoughts. How do you think happy thoughts? Ask yourself **Happy Power-Thinking questions.** Here are some examples:

- *If I'm feeling down, what five activities can I do to elevate me to a happier state of mind?*
- *How can I make it fun?*
- *What do I do that gives me a sense of purpose – a feeling of well-being?*
- *What's comical about that situation?*
- *What new thing can I create, learn, or accomplish today on my personal growth journey?*

Create and answer your own Happy Power-Thinking question.

In closing this happiness section, enjoy this personal poem which was taken from a speech I gave at Toastmasters.

HAPPINESS MADE SIMPLE

If you've been going through the motions of life,
Taking an apathetic "nappy,"
Then the first thing you must do to change direction,
Is decide you want to be happy.

You must alter your course 180 degrees,
Make a shift in emotional latitude,
Take action now with your second big step,
View the world with a positive attitude.

When you're taking yourself too seriously,
And life's been rough for quite a while,
Think happy thoughts to get you out of your rut,
Lighten up and laugh and smile.

When you dread a task or circumstance,
But it's something that must be done,
Approach it with this question in mind,
How can you make it fun?

Yes, it's OK to love yourself,
In a non-narcissistic way,
Healthy self-esteem on a daily basis,
Can help make for a happy day.

And physiologically speaking,
If you're slumping like a rubber band,
Simply act as if you're happy,
You'll be amazed how proud you stand.

My final bit of advice to you,
Be happy is step three,
Don't place limits on your happiness,
And very happy you will be.

Δ *Decide to be happy.*

Δ *Happiness is the process of*
   personal growth.

Δ *Flexible and creative thought*
   encourages happiness.

Δ *Lighten up! How can I make it fun?*

Creative Power Thinking

You are alive to the extent
you use your creative capabilities.

BILL MAYER

CREATIVE CALISTHENICS
AND MENTAL AEROBICS

By challenging your creative abilities – your ability to think originally – you can

- *"Aerobicise" your mind*
- *Stretch your imagination*
- *Exercise your inventiveness*
- *Limber up your mental agility*
- *Promote "originality muscle tone"*
- *Work out your right brain's resourcefulness*

You are alive, zestful, and passionate about life to the extent that you use your creative capabilities!

Creative Power Thinking applies to you productively using your creativity to improve the quality and vitality of your life and the lives of others. Creative Power Thinkers are **solution oriented** – they are always "exercising" their minds, searching for answers in creative ways. They are also flexible in their thinking, realizing that there is often more than one right answer to a problem. Creative Power Thinkers are persistent in asking and answering two specific questions: "What is a possible solution?" and "What is a better solution?"

EOVS

As the author of *The Magic in Asking the Right Questions*, I have to "walk my talk." I have to apply the principles that I teach. I regularly challenge myself to be creative in turning any of my negative viewpoints into positive ones.

I used to view my monthly bills with resentment. This made paying bills an unpleasant chore. I asked myself, "What's a more creative and empowering way of viewing my monthly bills?" My inner voice responded emphatically with three words – **Exchanges of Value.** I immediately referred to them as **EOVs.** I no longer view my bills as bills but rather as exchanges of value – valued money for valued service. How did this make me feel? Thankful!

Now, when I send off my payments – EOVs – to the phone company or whomever, I do it with an attitude of gratitude and appreciation. To reinforce this positive feeling, I often write *EOV = Thanks!* at the bottom of the checks I send out. Creativity can definitely help create happier emotional states.

Most "experts" agree that we use less than ten percent of our brain's mental capacity. Power Thinkers say "bah-humbug" to this notion and forge ahead by challenging their infinite creative capabilities.

How do you challenge your creative capabilities? By consistently asking yourself creatively challenging questions. **Creativity is stimulated by questions.** As a Power Thinker, it is important to master the skill of asking creative empowering questions and also to use your creative expertise to provide supportive empowering answers.

Challenging your creativity can put a spark of excitement into your life. I have a friend, Matthew, who was "sleeping his life away." He was going through the motions of life in a state of *numb.* He often complained about his life being boring and uninteresting. One day I had enough of his *gloom and doom* and communicated strongly to him, "If you're living a dull, boring, and uninteresting life, then guess what, Matthew? You're thinking dull, boring, and uninteresting thoughts!" He was momentarily stunned because rarely had he ever heard me raise my voice. He asked, "How can I change? How can I become more alive?"

I responded, "Challenge your creativity."

"What do you mean?" he questioned. "What do you think I mean?" I replied. He smiled and nodded his head. The process had started, and his creative juices began to flow. Ten creatively challenging questions later and Matthew was convinced that he no longer had to "sleep his life away."

Set aside a specific time daily to work out in the "gymnasium" called your mind. *Creative calisthenics and mental aerobics* are at least as important as pumping iron and running on the treadmill. If you want to live your life with zest, passion, and enthusiasm, you must continually challenge your creative capabilities.

To stimulate creativity, ask yourself **Creative Power-Thinking questions.** Here are some examples:

- *How can I provide better quality service to my customers?*
- *Can I visualize and describe in detail my dream home?*
- *How can I double my monthly income?*
- *What are ten ways I can let my partner know I love him/her?*
- *How can I make this product more marketable?*

Create and answer your own Creative Power-Thinking question.

Δ *Creativity inspires aliveness and vitality.*

Δ *Challenge your mind, stretch your imagination.*

Δ *Creative Power Thinkers are solution oriented.*

Δ *EOVs are exchanges of value.*

Δ *Creativity is stimulated by questions.*

Self-Esteem Power Thinking

There is no judgment a person can pass
that is more significant than
the one passed on him or herself,
no single factor more responsible
for the shape his or her life takes.

DR. NATHANIEL BRANDEN

YOU ARE THE "I" IN INTEGRITY

I ntegrity is a personal matter. What is integrity? It is when your external behavior and life you live corresponds with your self-professed inner values. This is the key to healthy self-esteem.

The degree to which you live in harmony with your values is the degree to which you will experience healthy, positive self-esteem.

What are values? They are the things that are most important to you in your life. What are some of your major values? Honesty? Love? Courage? Joy? Freedom? Security? Health? Adventure? Fun? Intelligence? It's been observed, "If you don't stand for something, you'll fall for anything." The surest way to establish and nurture healthy self-esteem is to write down a **Values Checklist** of at least ten values. How? Simply ask yourself, "What do I value most in my life?" List ten responses and then ask, "Do I live in harmony with these values?" Regarding healthy self-esteem, no truer words were ever spoken than William Shakespeare's, "To thine own self be true."

The following illustration is a sample Values Checklist. Take a moment to ponder what is most important in your life and then write down your ten most important values.

		DO I LIVE IN HARMONY WITH THIS VALUE?
1.	Family/Quality Time	✓
2.	Health/Vitality	◯
3.	Personal Growth/Happiness	✓
4.	Humor/Having Fun	✓
5.	Love/Compassion	◯
6.	Creativity/Resourcefulness	✓
7.	Integrity/Loving my Work	✓
8.	Success/Making a Difference	✓
9.	Adventure/New Challenges	◯
10.	Spiritual Connection/Quiet Time	✓

VALUES CHECKLIST

It's necessary to understand that there are **means** values and **ends** values. I asked a group of ten persons, "What's most important in your life? What motivates you?" Five of the ten persons responded, "Money – I'm money motivated." I tried to explain to them that money was actually a means to an end. I said, "It's not the money, the *means* value, that motivates you, but rather the *ends* value such as freedom, happiness, security, or power. These ends values are the end results of what you think money will provide you." I added, "How do these ends values make you feel?" When you write down your list of values, include only ends values because these are the most important to you.

Self-Esteem Power Thinkers are true to their values. They make better decisions because the choices they make are based on and in harmony with their values. When they're confused about a decision, they simply go down their Values Checklist and form a question with each value. For example: "Is this what a person with high **integrity** would do?" or "Is this what a **healthy** person would eat?"

THE "MANN" WITH INTEGRITY

A gentleman who I truly respect and admire is Ted Mann. If you looked up the definition of integrity in the dictionary, you would probably see a picture of Ted Mann. I had the pleasure and privilege of meeting him in 1988. He became one of my tennis students while visiting in San Diego, California. His backhand was questionable, but his integrity was perfect.

As I share this story with you, check your own integrity. When I first met Ted, he had recently sold his movie theater empire, Mann Theatres, for a substantial amount of money. On a Thursday afternoon, he was offered what he considered a "fair deal" to sell his business. He made a verbal agreement with this interested buyer, sealing it with a handshake. He "gave his word" that if their finances checked out okay and if they, in turn, were happy with the financial stability of Mann Theatres, that it was a done deal.

The very next day, Friday, Ted was offered an additional twenty million dollars by another prospective buyer. Talk about a dilemma – Wow! Ted said, "That weekend of soul searching and decision making was one of the toughest, most gut-wrenching two days of my life." On one side of the coin was his **integrity** and one of his greatest values was **honesty**. On the other side was twenty million dollars cash (time for your integrity check: Do you have twenty-million-dollar integrity?). He asked himself, "What would a person with impeccable integrity do in this situation?"

Monday morning Ted woke up with a smile – his decision had been made. He chose to stick by his "handshake deal" that he had verbally agreed to. It cost him twenty million dollars, but it didn't cost him his integrity. He felt good about his decision because it was based on his highest inner values. His healthy self-esteem got even healthier. I will always think of Ted as the "Mann with Integrity."

What does the profile of Self-Esteem Power Thinkers look like? Remember, self-esteem always comes from within. They exhibit the following qualities:

- **Self-acceptance** – Self-acceptance based on *internal standards*, not comparisons with others' abilities or achievements. They recognize and appreciate their own uniqueness. A Power Thinker's smile says, "I like and accept myself."
- **Self-confidence** – Strong sense of personal competence and ability to cope with the challenges of life. They have superior self-control and self-discipline and are often highly ambitious, innovative, and responsible. Self-Esteem Power Thinkers exhibit good posture and a self-assured presence.
- **Self-respect** – Sense of worthiness and self-approval attained by living in accordance with one's inner values. They respect who they are and what they stand for.
- **Happiness magnet** – Progressive personal growth journey ensures happiness. A Power Thinker's high self-esteem increases his or her inner capacity for happiness.
- **Respect for quality and excellence** – Life lived with the attitude, of "Be the best you can be!" Self-Esteem Power Thinkers recognize that the only way to get value is to give value.
- **Self-trust and self-love** – Ability to extend trust and love to others because of a solid foundation of trust and love in self. These Power Thinkers like and feel good about themselves from the inside out.

MIRROR IMAGE

Self-esteem – how you feel about yourself – affects every aspect of your life. As a Power Thinker, having high self-esteem influences your life in a positive way and is one of the most important ingredients to all-lasting success. How you view the world and interact with fellow human beings is a *mirror image* of how you feel about yourself. Healthy self-respect breeds kindness, generosity, and respect for others. Self-acceptance allows you to more readily accept others, without passing judgment. Self-love and self-trust open the door for true love and unshakable trust in your intimate relationships.

SELF-TALK

Your self-esteem is sculptured by your self-talk – how you talk to and evaluate yourself on a daily basis. Your self-talk is the chisel that can shape a self-esteem "masterpiece" or create a self-esteem "bust." Either way, the resulting feeling you have about yourself will govern and regulate your behavior.

Negative, destructive, disempowering self-talk results in negative, destructive, disempowering behavior. Self-talk of "stupid," "jerk," or "loser" will guarantee you a below par, insecure performance and low self-esteem. Positive, constructive, empowering self-talk will result in positive, constructive, empowering behavior. Self-talk of "good job," "well done," or "excellent" will encourage a better, more confident performance and higher self-esteem.

As a Power Thinker, you strengthen your self-esteem daily by mastering the art of self-talk. You are constantly aware of and can selectively control the information you put into your conscious mind. To override your subconscious mind's past negative conditioning, you must consciously and relentlessly fill your mind with positive empowering thoughts, affirmations, and values about yourself that will support you in the direction you want to go with your life. There is power in imagining yourself as the person you want to become.

How do you do this? Take a guess. You're right again – Self-Esteem Power-Thinking questions. Here are some examples:

- *What am I proud about in my life right now? In what areas do I want to become more competent?*
- *What do I have a problem accepting about myself? How can I change this?*
- *What's most important on my personal growth journey?*
- *What would have to happen for me to smile more often? And how can I improve my self-talk?*
- *How can I give more value to my clients?*

Create and answer your own Self-Esteem Power-Thinking question.

If you haven't already done so, ask yourself the most important of all self-esteem questions, "What are the ten things I value most in life?" Then ask, "Do I live in harmony with these values?"

Take the time to write them down – you're worth it!

Δ *You are the "I" in integrity.*

Δ *Healthy self-esteem means living*
    in harmony with your values.

Δ *Self-esteem is self-acceptance,*
    self-confidence, self-respect, self-trust,
    and self-love.

Δ *Be the best you can be!*

Δ *To master self-talk, consciously affirm*
    how you want to be.

Positive Power Thinking

Any fact facing us
is not as important as our attitude toward it,
for that determines our success or failure.

NORMAN VINCENT PEALE

POSITIVELY EXPECTANT

Being *positively expectant* means already having a picture in your mind's eye of a positive outcome. This is the single greatest attribute of Positive Power Thinkers. They know that life is a self-fulfilling prophecy and people usually get what they expect, so they **expect the best** in every situation.

Positive Power Thinkers' attitudes are not determined by external circumstances, but rather how they *choose* to respond to those circumstances. Shakespeare accurately surmised, "There is nothing either good or bad, but thinking makes it so." Power Thinkers recognize their freedom to choose whether to react positively or negatively to a situation; their glass is always half full not half empty. As a Positive Power Thinker, your strength lies in your positive viewpoint.

Understand that it's not what happens in your life that's important so much as your interpretation of what happens.

Mother Teresa is definitely a Positive Power Thinker. Her interpretation or viewpoint of what happens in her life is remarkable. One day at the airport she was approached by a stressful traveling companion who said, "We have a problem with our flight." Mother Teresa responded, "There are no problems, only gifts. There are small gifts, and there are big gifts. Which are you offering?" Her friend exclaimed, "Our flight is going to be at least two hours late!" Mother Teresa calmly communicated, "That would be a small gift. What a wonderful opportunity to finish reading the novel I started yesterday."

Remember, it's not what happens in your life that's important so much as your interpretation of what happens.

Positive Power Thinkers know they can't always control their circumstances, but they can control and determine their own thoughts.

It's comforting to know that ultimately, with your positive viewpoint, you can be at *cause over* your thoughts and consequent feelings – and not the *effect of* an unpleasant event or circumstance.

Positive Power Thinkers also transform their lives by turning negatives into positives. How? They listen to their inner dialogue of thoughts, and if these thoughts are negative and disempowering, they "short-circuit" and interrupt them by

1. *Proclaiming, "Stop! This thought is totally unacceptable!"*
2. *Then asking themselves, "What's a better, more empowering way of viewing this situation?"*
3. *And, finally, using the answer as a positive affirmation to direct their lives.*

It really is as simple as one-two-three.

Use the analogy of the traffic signal in the following illustration to help clarify how you can short-circuit your negative thoughts and turn them into positive ones.

RED	STOP!	*The negative thought*
YELLOW	CAUTION.	*Ask yourself a positive empowering question*
GREEN	GO!	*Forward with your positive affirmation*

Now let's see if this stop-and-go technique is as simple as one-two-three. Susan was learning the tennis serve. She was having trouble putting it all together and was getting frustrated. After throwing her ball toss five feet behind herself, she proclaimed, "I'm so uncoordinated, I'll never get this!" Realizing her disempowering statement, she said, "Stop, this is a totally unacceptable thought!" She asked herself, "What's a better way of looking at this situation?" Her response, which she used as a positive affirmation was, "My ball placement is getting better with each practice toss – I can do this!" Within a week Susan went from hitting less than ten percent of her serves into the service box to having success over fifty percent of the time. Most importantly, she was steadily gaining confidence and was inspired to play more often.

Selectively appreciative focus means choosing to focus on things that you are thankful for. Positive Power Thinkers choose to be *appreciative*. They live their life with an attitude of gratitude and openly express their thank-yous. They've mastered the skill of *selectively focusing* on what they like and appreciate in life. They have a conscious, grateful awareness passionately living out the lyrics of an old hymn, "Count your blessings, name them one by one." Positive Power Thinkers are eternal optimists. Their viewpoints concur with Emerson, "When it gets dark enough, you can see the stars."

What's the best way to guide your thinking process and life into a more positive and appreciative direction? Would you believe **Positive Power-Thinking questions?** Here are some examples:

- *What am I thankful for in my life right now?*
- *What qualities do I like most about _____ (fill in a name)?*
- *What's great about this situation?*
- *How can I turn this problem into an opportunity?*
- *Who do I appreciate most in my life right now? Why?*

Create and answer your own Positive Power-Thinking question.

△ *Expect the best.*

△ *Choose to have a positive attitude.*

△ *Short-circuit the negative,*
  ask an empowering question,
  and then affirm the positive.

△ *Focus on what you're grateful for.*

Responsible Power Thinking

*Man must cease attributing his problems
to his environment, and
learn again to exercise his will –
his personal responsibility.*

ALBERT SCHWEITZER

EXCUSE-ITIS

Excuse-itis is a disease of the irresponsible. Stanley's life was one big excuse. After his last tennis defeat, he was overheard mumbling, "It was too windy, too sunny, and I only got a few hours sleep last night." As he was being fired from his most recent job, he complained, "My boss was too demanding, and my health benefits weren't any good." At his divorce proceedings, he lamented, "My wife doesn't know how to communicate, and she doesn't have a clue about saving money." His life was miserable because he refused to accept responsibility for anything in his life. Do you know anybody like Stanley?

Excuse-itis is not in the makeup of Responsible Power Thinkers – they do not make excuses. Responsible Power Thinkers assume one hundred percent responsibility for everything that has happened or will ever happen in their lives. They do not blame parents, government, bosses, or external circumstances for who or where they are, but rather accept total responsibility for the conditions in their life. Simply put, they are **personally accountable** for their life.

MAJOR ATTRIBUTES OF RESPONSIBLE POWER THINKERS

- **Positive self-control** – Responsible Power Thinkers take responsibility for causing the effects in their own lives. They are in control because they, not others, make the *decisions* in their lives. Remember, thoughts are causes – and results and behaviors are effects – so it's also taking responsibility for what they think.
- **Action orientation** – Responsible Power Thinkers take initiative, constantly looking for ways to impact and improve their lives. Through actions, their attitude of self-responsibility is implemented and expressed. They're productive, achieving players – not passive, vicarious spectators in the game of life. They *make it happen* because they're in control.
- **Self-reliance** – They trust in their own abilities and depend on themselves to direct their own lives. They're answerable under all circumstances to me, myself, and I.
- **Definitive decision makers** – Why? Because Responsible Power Thinkers know where they're going; they're in the driver's seat of their lives. Responsible equals decisive; irresponsible equals indecisive.

- **Efficient time managers** – Why? Because they avoid procrastination. How? By affirming, "I do it now!" They recognize time as precious.
- **Effective emotional-state managers** – Higher acceptance of responsibility means more control. More control means personal freedom to choose and experience positive emotions. Blame and other negative emotions can be stopped by affirming, "I am responsible!"
- **High self-esteem** – There is a direct correlation between high levels of responsibility and high levels of self-esteem and happiness.

CHOOSE TO BE RESPONSIBLE

Do you want to be at *cause* and in control of your life, or at e*ffect* and out of control? Do you want to have a victim consciousness, or an accountability consciousness? Do you want to be dependable and trustworthy, or unreliable and lacking in trust? Do you want to be procrastination oriented, or action oriented? Do you want to be responsible and decisive, or irresponsible and indecisive?

The bottom line is that responsibility is a matter of choice, so choose to be responsible!

Arbie M. Dale, clinical psychologist, concurs, "To decide, to be at a level of choice, is to take responsibility for your life and be in control of your life." Who is going to be the master decision maker in your life?

Challenge yourself to become more responsible. How? Ask, and then answer, **Responsible Power-Thinking questions**. Here are some examples:

- *What specific actions should I take to be more productive at work?*
- *What's the best use of my time right now?*
- *How can I become more responsible in paying my bills on time?*
- *What important project have I been putting off? What am I going to do to get jump-started?*
- *What have I been irresponsible about in my life? What action am I going to take to make a change?*

Create and answer your own Responsible Power-Thinking question.

- Δ *No excuses!*
- Δ *Choose to be responsible.*
- Δ *Be one hundred percent personally accountable.*
- Δ *Procrastination? Say to yourself, "I do it now!"*
- Δ *Blame? Tell yourself, "I am responsible!"*

Healthy Power Thinking

Disease and health,

like circumstances,

are rooted in thought.

JAMES ALLEN

PSYCHOSOMATIC OPTIMAL HEALTH

The term *psychosomatic optimal health* exemplifies the positive mind-set of a Healthy Power Thinker. It implies that a positive psyche (mind) will contribute to producing a healthy, vibrant, and energized soma (body). Healthy Power Thinkers know that the body is the servant of the mind, and that unhealthy thoughts create disease and illness, and healthy thoughts encourage vitality, vigor, and soundness of mind and body.

Healthy Power Thinkers effectively manage stress. They know that fear, worry, and anxiety are created by *negative expectations* – expecting the worst result in a given situation. These negative emotions can cause hypertension, ulcers, strokes, and many other physical illnesses. How do they effectively manage stress? Most importantly, they are aware that stress and tension are not contained in circumstances or events, but rather stress and tension arise from their **reactions** to circumstances or events. Controlling their conscious minds, Healthy Power Thinkers can control in a more positive way their reactions to different circumstances, events, or situations in their life. They do this by asking themselves questions that are *positively expectant* – questions which when answered will create a positive desirable outcome. As a result, stress and tension are reduced or sometimes completely eliminated.

SOLUTION ORIENTED = STRESS REDUCTION

Your viewpoint and consequent stress level will be affected by the questions you ask yourself. Let's look at how Wally Worry and Sammy Solution deal with the same potentially stressful situation. They both have identical middle-class incomes, and they both owe $20,000 in credit-card bills.

Wally asks himself a disempowering question, "How am I ever going to get out from under this overwhelming mountain of debt?" Worry, anxiety, and stress are magnified by hopeless questions like this. The *negatively expectant* implication of this question is that he may never get out of debt. This will definitely raise his stress level!

In contrast, Sammy asks himself an empowering question, "What specific actions do I need to take to pay off these credit cards?" This question is *positively expectant* in nature, as it implies that his bills will be paid off if he takes specific action.

Because it is **solution oriented**, this question will lessen or even eliminate any potential stress and tension.

Remember, the quality of your life, especially your health, is determined by the quality of the questions you ask yourself on a daily basis.

ENERGIZED ALIVENESS

Psychosomatic optimal health is not just the absence of disease; it is an energized aliveness! Healthy Power Thinkers live with zest, enthusiasm, and a passion for life. They're consciously filling their minds with healthy, positive, empowering thoughts to create a healthy, energized, and alive body. Happy, strong, and pure thoughts will help build and nourish a healthy body.

PURIFY MIND – PURIFY BODY

Healthy Power Thinkers pay attention to their diet, especially monitoring their fatty food, sugar, caffeine, and alcohol intake. James Allen, author of *As a Man Thinketh,* wisely observed that this is not enough. He proclaimed, "Change of diet will not help a man who will not change his thoughts. When a man makes his thoughts pure, he no longer desires impure food." I took his advice, and it works.

H₂O AND O₂ POWER

Healthy Power Thinkers understand and utilize the power of water and oxygen. Seventy percent of the earth's surface is water. Seventy percent of your body is water. Is this a coincidence? Healthy Power Thinkers take nature's hint and cleanse, nourish, and purify their bodies by drinking a lot of water. How much water should you have and in what form? Drink at least half of your body weight in fluid ounces every day. For example, if you weigh one hundred and fifty pounds, drink at least seventy-five ounces of water. Bottled, filtered, and distilled water are best. Also, consume at least fifty percent of your overall diet in water-soluble foods, like fruits and vegetables, which *cleanse,* not *clog,* your body.

Healthy Power Thinkers know that oxygen is the major source of energy for their minds and bodies. They breathe regularly and deeply. A healthy way to energize yourself daily is to do deep *diaphragmatic breathing* exercises. This type of breathing utilizes the strong muscular action between the chest and abdominal cavities to oxygenate and energize your mind and body at a cellular level.

To apply this effective breathing technique, do the following three steps:

1. *Inhale and take a deep breath*
2. *Hold it for ten seconds*
3. *Exhale for five seconds*

Do ten deep breaths whenever you need to be energized. Simply remember the two-to-one ratio of holding your breath to exhaling. Another example:

1. *Inhale deeply*
2. *Hold for sixteen seconds*
3. *Exhale for eight seconds*

Experiment and see what specific number of seconds in this two-to-one ratio energizes you most. Healthy Power Thinkers also oxygenate their minds and bodies a minimum of twenty consecutive minutes, three times a week, with an aerobic activity. Walking, hiking, running, swimming, skiing, and biking are examples of good aerobic exercises. They are also excellent "endorphin-high" outlets, which help to alleviate anger, worry, and other stress-inducing negative emotions.

LOVE IS BLISSFUL

Healthy Power Thinkers are loving in nature. They know that to think well of and to be cheerful to all, to look for the good in everyone, to be kind, considerate, unselfish, and accepting of others is going to produce peace of mind, a calm nervous system, and an optimal healthy body. Healthy Power Thinkers often have a spiritual side that they tap into by spending some quality "quiet time" daily. This could be through the experience of meditation or simply taking a warm, peaceful bath. Serenity and bliss are just a few healthy, loving, and peaceful thoughts away.

If you want to think healthy empowering thoughts, then ask **Healthy Power-Thinking questions.** Yes, there is magic in asking the right questions. Here are some examples:

- *What's the best way to handle my anger? My worry? My fear?*
- *What are three actions I can take to immediately raise my energy level?*
- *What foods do I need to eliminate in order to lower my cholesterol level?*
- *What are three types of activities I enjoy that would aerobicise my body?*
- *What do I like about _____ (fill in a name)?*

Create and answer your own Healthy Power-Thinking question.

Δ *Health and disease originate with thought.*

Δ *A positively expectant viewpoint helps effectively manage stress.*

Δ *Purifying your mind will help purify your body.*

Δ *Cleanse and energize yourself with H_2O and O_2 power.*

Δ *Loving thoughts equal peaceful mind and healthy body.*

Prosperity Power Thinking

Wealth is the product
of man's capacity to think.

AYN RAND

PROSPERITY CONSCIOUSNESS

You've got to believe, with unshakable confidence, that you can and will achieve your financial goals. Prosperity Power Thinkers understand that all monetary riches start in the mind, and it *is* possible to think and grow rich. Everything you ever have in life, including the accumulation of wealth, is a direct result of how you use your mind. Improve the quality of your financial thinking, and you will improve the quality and quantity of your financial success in life.

The very first step in becoming a Prosperity Power Thinker is to **decide you want to be wealthy.** Believe it or not, many people never choose to make this decision.

As a Prosperity Power Thinker, you would –

- Confidently expect to be wealthy.
- Consciously take control of your thoughts by making them consistent with your *desire for financial abundance* and removing any *fears of lack of money*. Remember, "You become what you think about." Your thoughts of *lack* will lead to *poverty*, and your thoughts of *abundance* will lead to *wealth*. Your self-talk affirms regularly and with conviction – "I earn at least $10,000 a month" or "I am a millionaire!" or whatever your monetary objective is.
- Visualize financial independence with frequency, emotional intensity, and clarity. Visualization stimulates the unlimited powers of your subconscious mind. Clarity equals power; that is, increased vividness equals stronger forces pulling you toward financial independence.
- Become wealthy by seeing what others want and need, and then providing a product or service of superior value to fulfill that need. The creative idea to fulfill a need, when acted upon, creates your money flow.

Fred Smith is a Prosperity Power Thinker. Through extensive market research while at college he discovered a *need* in the mailing industry. His vision was to fulfill this need by providing a prompt, dependable, overnight delivery service. He even wrote a thesis about his vision, and his dream research paper received a grade of F – flunk! Even though his college professor did not duplicate his enthusiasm, Fred persisted and created Federal Express. His company is now a member, in good standing, of the "Forbes 100 Club" and has assets approaching ten billion dollars.

Fred Smith saw a need, created a means to fulfill that need, took action on it, and is now a multimillionaire. It all started with one man's creative idea. Ayn Rand, author and philosopher, was accurate – "Wealth *is* the product of man's capacity to think."

MONEY MAGNET

Typically, financial abundance of Prosperity Power Thinkers comes from doing what they *love to do*. They are clear about their goals and flexible about the process of attaining them. Their money flow is often a by-product of pursuing their *passion*. They put a minimum of ten percent of their gross income into savings each month.

Prosperity Power Thinkers give generously of their money, because they understand that the *vacuum* this creates in the universe will attract more money. They derive their greatest pleasures and financial rewards by creating tremendous value and fulfilling the desires and needs of others. By doing what they love to do and relentlessly filling their conscious minds with thoughts, words, and images of their desired wealth, Prosperity Power Thinkers become "money magnets." They attract people, circumstances, and opportunities into their lives that ensure them financial success. This strengthens their belief, confidence, and knowingness of creating and maintaining their personal fortunes.

Prosperity is just an abundant thought away – maybe a few thousand abundant thoughts away – so get started now!

How do you think prosperously? Ask **Prosperity Power-Thinking questions.** Here are some examples:

- *What specific annual income do I need to generate in order to live abundantly, not just comfortably?*
- *What negative or painful beliefs do I have about money that hold me back from achieving my financial goals?*
- *What are the benefits of doubling my monthly income?*
- *What specific actions do I need to take to pay off all my credit cards and save a minimum of ten percent of my earnings?*
- *Do I always go the extra mile to ensure that I give extra value in the service I provide for others? If yes, great! If no, what can I do to improve?*

Create and answer your own Prosperity Power-Thinking question.

Δ *All riches originate in the mind.*

Δ *Decide on and then confidently expect wealth.*

Δ *Consciously control your thoughts with desires of abundance.*

Δ *Visualize financial independence.*

Δ *Be a giver and always provide extra value.*

Simplified Power Thinking

Genius is the ability
to reduce the complicated
to the simple.

C. W. CERM

SIMPLIFY AND APPLY

Simplified Power Thinkers have the wisdom to recognize and utilize the power of simplicity. They simplify – to clarify – and then apply.

Simplify means to make less complex, more clear

and understandable.

Apply means to take action on that simplified knowledge.

As a Power Thinker, how do you simplify? By first asking, then answering, a Simplified Power-Thinking question – and finally taking action. Ask yourself, "How can I simplify this?" Follow your answer to this question with, "How can I apply this?"

Sounds simple – doesn't it? Yes, but don't let this mislead you, because it also is very powerful! To support this concept, look at what wise men of the past have said about simplicity.

*The ability to simplify means
to eliminate the unnecessary,
so that the necessary may speak.*

HANS HOFFMAN

---

*All great truths are simple in final analysis,
and easily understood;
if they are not, they are not great truths.*

NAPOLEON HILL

---

*The obvious is that which is never seen until
someone expresses it simply.*

KAHLIL GIBRAN

Clearness is the ornament of profound thought.

MARQUIS DE VAUVENARGUES

---

*It is a simple task to make things complex,
but a complex task to make them simple.*

MAYER'S LAW

When I first learned the backhand stroke in tennis, I was told three specific things to do by my coach. He instructed, "Put your *thumb* behind the grip for more support, pull your racquet *back*, feeling your elbow in at your stomach for efficiency, and *throw* your arm to the net, leading with the racquet head." Feeling somewhat overwhelmed with this new information, I asked myself, "How can I simplify this?" My response was three words, "Thumb, Back, Throw." Next I asked myself, "How can I apply this new simplified knowledge?" My answer, "Use a ball machine." So I took my three *buzz words* out on the court and hit hundreds, if not thousands, of backhand practice strokes. Within two weeks my backhand was better than my forehand and to this day it still is.

I eventually simplified the buzz words of "Thumb, Back, Throw" to TBT. When you break down the complex into simple parts, then no challenge is too difficult.

Here are some other examples of **Simplified Power-Thinking questions:**

- *How can I communicate it more clearly?*
- *What's an easier way to get from point A to point B?*
- *How can I make this information more understandable?*

Create and answer your own Simplified Power-Thinking question.

Δ *Simplify to clarify and then apply.*

Δ *Understanding comes from simplifying the complex.*

Δ *A key to mental mastery is simplicity.*

CHAPTER 4

Power Communications:
Choose Better Words

Without knowing the force of words
it is impossible to know men.

CONFUCIUS

BIGGER IS NOT NECESSARILY BETTER

Power Thinkers do not try to impress and distance you
with the size of their words, but rather develop rapport
with you by the choice of their words. They realize that
just as their thoughts are a matter of choice, so are the words
they convey inwardly in self-talk, or outwardly to a fellow
human being in conversation. As a result, the Power Thinker's
motto regarding communication is "Think before you speak,"
actually – "Power Think before you speak."

Power Thinkers don't put friends, co-workers, or
acquaintances on the defensive because their choice of words
are supportive rather than attacking in nature. Leo was having
personal problems, and his work reflected this. His productivity had been cut in half. Roger, Leo's boss and a Power Thinker,

communicated to him, "I'm **concerned about** your performance." He spent a few minutes conveying what his concerns were. He could have just as easily said, "I'm **bothered by** your performance," and gotten off on what bothered him. By choosing more supportive words, *concerned about* versus *bothered by*, Roger was able to maintain rapport with Leo at a time when he needed a little empathy. Two weeks later, Leo was back on track reaching his productivity goals. Roger's compassionate choice of words was just a small part in Leo turning things around, but it was helpful. It pays to take the time and effort to choose better, more supportive words.

If asked to constructively criticize, Power Thinkers' suggestions are always directed toward the individual's *behavior*, not toward the individual. Power Thinkers believe that *how* something is communicated is just as important as *what* is communicated. The intended meaning in most communications is more likely to be duplicated if it is nonthreatening.

WORD POWER

Words influence and shape your beliefs and impact your actions. Words have power, and this power can be negative or positive. Therefore, your words must be chosen wisely. As a Power Thinker, choose to eliminate limiting self-talk words, such as *if only, should, ought to, but, can't, try, doubt, failure,* and *impossible.* These words are destructive and nonsupportive in shaping your destiny. If you want to improve your communication with yourself and others, and ultimately improve the quality of your life, you must consciously select to use supportive and empowering words and continually aim to improve your level of choice.

Words convey not only literal meaning, but create mental pictures and emotional intensity. You can be a *master* or a *slave* to your words and the emotional states they create. "Word-slaves" typically have restricted vocabularies and communicate in a reactive unconscious state of mind. Their habitual *limiting self-talk* makes them prisoners to their own words. They are slaves to the disempowering words they often use, which trigger and then lock them into their negative emotions. On the contrary are Power-Thinking "word-masters" who typically command extensive vocabularies and communicate in a present-time conscious state of mind. Word-masters' skillful use of empowering words make them champions over the positive emotions that these words help to create.

As a Power Thinker, you become more aware of any negative ideas you might communicate to yourself or to others. You immediately short-circuit your negative thoughts by asking yourself, "What is a better choice of words that I can substitute, which is more positive and supportive?" Simply put, **"What's a better, more empowering way to express this?"** Use your creative imagination – the more fun and outrageous you are in creating better, more empowering word choices, the more likely you will short-circuit your disempowering words. This will help to weaken or eliminate the pain inflicted by any negative emotions these words might have created. For example, "I'm *learning a lesson*" is not nearly as painful as, "I'm a *failure.*" Refer to the Choosing Better Words illustration to clarify this concept.

DIS-EMPOWERING WORDS CREATE _Negative Emotions_	EMPOWERING WORDS CREATE _Positive Emotions_
Confused ·····················➤	Sorting Things Out
Depressed ····················➤	Temporarily Feeling Down
Failure ·······················➤	Learning a Lesson
Fearful ·······················➤	Aroused
Frustrated ····················➤	Fascinated
Irritated ·····················➤	Stimulated
Nervous ······················➤	Energized
Overwhelmed ················➤	Challenged
Pathetic ·····················➤	Unique
Scared ·······················➤	Excited

CHOOSING BETTER WORDS

TEMPORARY NEGATIVE EMOTION

The degree to which you feel pain with a negative emotion can be decreased by selecting a better word. By consciously selecting a better word, you get out of the painful web that your subconscious mind wants to keep you trapped in. Sometimes my creative mind decides to shut down for the day and my capacity for choosing better words is diminished. On these occasions I simply put the word _temporarily_ in front of any negative emotion I'm experiencing. For example, if I'm angry, I will say, "I'm temporarily angry," since this implies that I'm not _stuck in_, but rather, _in transition toward_ feeling better. It also lightens up the situation which makes a positive emotion more accessible.

Physiologically, words have an astounding impact on your body. The words that you associate with your experience become your *perceived experience* and stimulate sensations produced by your nervous system. Depressed thoughts and words will round out your shoulders, cause your movements to be slower, and direct your eyes downward. Enthusiastic thoughts will improve your posture, put a bounce in your step, and a twinkle in your eyes.

The amazing power of words is that they can also profoundly affect your emotional state. This is why it is essential to consciously develop and utilize a Power Thinker's vocabulary. By habitually using empowering words that are sending positive messages to your mind and body, your emotional state stands a much greater chance of becoming more positive.

SUPERLATIVE RESPONSES

Ralph and Cindy are fellow gym members who are at different ends of the spectrum when it comes to their choice of words and their choice of emotional states. I asked them both the identical question, "How are you feeling?" Ralph's typical responses are, "I'm getting by, I'm okay, or I'm fine." His most favorite is, "Not bad." I could never quite figure out what "not bad" means.

Cindy's responses are always more inspiring. As a Power Thinker, Cindy understands that **the degree to which you feel pleasure with a positive emotion can be enhanced by selecting a better, more empowering word to describe your emotion.**

She proudly admits that she sometimes gets carried away expressing how she feels. A sample of her superlative responses are, "I'm feeling awesome, confident, dynamite, ecstatic, energized, extraordinary, fabulous, fantastic, focused, incredible, invincible, magical, phenomenal, spectacular, terrific, vibrant!"

Which one of these two, Ralph or Cindy, do you think walks around the gym with good posture, a bounce in each step, and twinkling eyes? Superlative responses are actually affirmations of how you would truly like to feel. If some of these inspiring responses are too unnatural or uncomfortable for you, simply respond, "I'm feeling okay, and I'm moving toward feeling terrific!" Use your imagination and have fun being creative with your superlative responses.

WORD FOR THE DAY

I always admired how quickly and accurately my Mom could do crossword puzzles. After watching her complete the *New York Times* crossword puzzle in about twenty minutes, I asked her, "How did you get so good and so fast?" She responded, "Growing up I challenged myself to learn one new word every day. It became a habit, and over time I ended up with a very diverse and extensive vocabulary."

As a Power Thinker, make it a habit to learn one new word every day as part of your personal growth journey. There is a correlation between success in life and having an expanded vocabulary. Write down your word for the day on a three-by-five index card and refer to it periodically throughout the day. Each time you Rate Your State, you could glance at it. To understand its definition, apply your word for the day in more than one sentence. Make it fun, and you will develop a very healthy, positive, and useful habit.

AWARENESS OF WORD CHOICES

If you want to direct your life in a more positive manner, then you need to consciously evaluate and improve your habitual vocabulary. Make sure that it is propelling you in the direction you desire to go. How? By getting back to the basics, that is, the magic in asking the right questions. In review, two questions that I've found to be effective are "What's a better, more empowering way to express this?" and "What's a word that I can substitute that will lessen the intensity of the negative emotion or heighten the intensity of the positive emotion?" For example, substitute the word *challenged* for the word *overwhelmed.*

 As a Power Thinker, become more aware of the words you choose in speaking to yourself and others and continually aim to improve your level of choice in the words you do use. By consciously choosing better, more empowering words, you will inevitably improve your communication skills and your life.

Words are very powerful. Regarding one of the central themes of this book, we discover the following by replacing the word *thoughts* with the word *words* –

   Δ *Your words control your life (destiny).*
   Δ *You can control (choose) your words.*
   Δ *You can control your destiny.*

Δ *Power Think before you speak.*

Δ *To develop rapport, choose your words wisely.*

Δ *Words are powerful and can significantly impact your emotional states.*

Δ *Improve your vocabulary – make learning one new word per day a habit.*

Δ *Improve your communication skills and your life by consciously choosing to use better, more empowering words.*

CHAPTER 5

Believe in Your Power of Belief

Your belief
that you can do the thing
gives your thought
forces their power.

ROBERT COLLIER

YOU'VE GOT TO BELIEVE!

B elief is certainty of thought. It is a "gut-level knowingness" that whatever you undertake you will accomplish. Belief is expectant faith; you expect an outcome, positive or negative, before it actually occurs. Thoughts are powerful – thoughts with belief are more powerful – beliefs with conviction are most powerful. Convictions are strongest because of your increased emotional intensity and increased certainty associated with your beliefs.

Beliefs control your decisions and impact your emotions and actions and ultimate destiny. If you want to change your destiny, you must change your conscious thoughts, beliefs, and convictions, for they are the foundation of your life.

How do you make these changes? First of all, you have to figure out where you want to *ideally* go with your life – your ultimate destiny. This destiny is created by referring back to your Be-Do-Have goals list. Review your list of ten items each of how you want to be, what you wish to do, and what you desire to have.

Take time to also locate and review your Values Checklist. When you compare your values list with your goals list, you will more than likely see some cross-over. Basically, your Be goals are **feelings you value**, your Do goals are **actions you value**, and your Have goals are **possessions you value**.

You have disempowering and empowering beliefs associated with each one of your Be-Do-Have goals. Disempowering beliefs are any beliefs that take you away from your desired goals and ultimate destiny. Empowering beliefs are beliefs that move you toward your desired goals and ultimate destiny. Refer to the following illustration to clarify this concept.

ULTIMATE
DESTINY

Empowering beliefs **move you toward** *your ultimate destiny.*
Disempowering beliefs **take you away** *from your ultimate destiny.*

As a Power Thinker, to reach your ultimate destiny, you need to take two actions. First, you must recognize your disempowering beliefs – which weaken you – and eliminate them. Then, you must acknowledge your present, or create new, empowering beliefs – which strengthen you – and affirm them.

DISEMPOWERING AND EMPOWERING BELIEFS

Matthew was focusing on his financial goals. At the top of the list was his desire to earn $5,000 per month. His present income was half this amount – $2,500. He asked, "What are my disempowering beliefs regarding prosperity?" His immediate responses were, "I can't keep up with my bills!" and "I'm not worthy of making that much money!" Matthew remembered that to be an effective Power Thinker he needed to short-circuit his negative disempowering beliefs and replace them with empowering beliefs. These are essentially affirmations. He did this by declaring, "Stop! These are totally unacceptable beliefs!" He also associated pain and suffering with these limiting beliefs to short-circuit them more abruptly.

Matthew then replaced his old disempowering beliefs. His new empowering beliefs were, "I easily pay my monthly bills and have an abundance of money left over to fulfill other desires" and "I am totally worthy of earning $5,000 per month as I provide a valuable service to others." When your empowering beliefs are aligned with your goals and values, you will be unstoppable!

TRANSFORM BELIEFS INTO CONVICTIONS

There will be times in your life when it is beneficial to consciously transform your beliefs into convictions. The emotional intensity and passion of your convictions can inspire you to act in areas of your life where your basic beliefs may not have compelled you enough to have taken action.

Convictions are a *level of certainty* above beliefs. Therefore the first action you must take in transforming your beliefs into convictions is to strengthen your beliefs. To add certainty to your beliefs, ask yourself "reinforcing questions." These questions, when answered, will support, strengthen, and reinforce your basic beliefs. There is power in certainty, and with this increased certainty comes conviction.

Elizabeth was of the opinion and now the belief, "To be successful in life, you must focus your undivided attention on one specialized field of endeavor." **Step one** in transforming her belief into a conviction was **asking herself a reinforcing question.** She asked, "Who are some role models who support this belief?" Elizabeth came up with half a dozen famous persons concurring with her belief about the importance of focus. Her favorite quote was by Thomas Edison. He said, "If they took the time in question and applied it in one direction, to one object, they would succeed." Each of her role models' supportive quotes strengthened and reinforced her belief and increased her certainty.

Step two in her transformation process was for Elizabeth to **turn up the emotional intensity** of her belief a notch. She did this by asking one emotion-evoking question of pain and one emotion-evoking question of pleasure. Her pain question was, "What will it cost me in money, happiness, and self-esteem if I don't focus my undivided attention on one specialized field?" Her pleasure question was, "What benefits will I derive from focusing my undivided attention on one specialized field of endeavor?" Her responses to these questions increased her emotional intensity and propelled her into action.

Action, that is, taking action, is the third and final step of turning beliefs into convictions. As a computer technician, Elizabeth decided to take action by signing up for a computer class at a local university. She focused specifically on becoming an expert on the Internet as she saw herself most marketable in this specialized computer field. By taking action, she strengthened her commitment to her "power in focus" belief and raised her level of emotional intensity and conviction.

FEAR OF FAILURE

Limiting beliefs are often an accumulation of little failures that become a failure habit. This is then generalized into the biggest disempowering belief of all – the fear of failure – which translates into "I can't!"

To overcome failures, they must be viewed as temporary, specific to just a portion of your life, and not personal. *Not personal* means that a behavior or approach failed, not you. Failure is disempowering when viewed in terms of "I'm hopeless" or "There's no way this can be done!" Failure is empowering when viewed in terms of "What did I learn from this situation?" In answering this question, you can make positive distinctions and adjustments in your next approach and be one step closer to your desired outcome.

WHAT DID I LEARN FROM THIS?

Nelson Boswell, author of *Successful Living Day by Day*, observed, "The difference between greatness and mediocrity is often how an individual views a mistake." Malcolm S. Forbes, entrepreneur, concurs, "Failure is success if we learn from it."

How you deal with failure in your life will shape your destiny more than almost anything else.

If you fail at something, be sure to ask yourself these two questions, "What did I learn from this?" and "What will I do differently next time?" Taking action is imperative, because action conquers fear and can help you to re-establish your empowering beliefs.

Δ *Belief is certainty of thought.*
   Conviction is emotionally
   intensified belief.
Δ *Beliefs control your decisions and*
   impact your emotions and actions.
Δ *Eliminate your disempowering beliefs.*
Δ *Reinforce your empowering beliefs.*
Δ *Overcome failure by asking,*
   "What did I learn from this?"

CHAPTER 6

The Mastery of Mental Laws

Ideas are, in truth, forces.

HENRY JAMES

INVISIBLE BECOMES INVINCIBLE!

Just as there are physical laws of the universe, there are also mental laws that, although invisible, are in force and applicable one hundred percent of the time. Whenever you live in harmony – that is, your thoughts and actions are aligned with these invisible laws – your life will seem more balanced, peaceful, and *under control.* Whenever you violate any of these laws, your life will seem more disoriented, confused, and *out of control.*

There are numerous mental laws, all of which serve a specific purpose. The following are the four most significant laws that are essential to building a solid foundation for a Power Thinker's mental mastery:

THE FOUR LAWS OF MENTAL MASTERY

Law of Attraction

Law of Expectations

Law of Correspondence

Law of Cause and Effect

APPLY THE LAWS

Understanding these mental laws will help propel you to be all you want to be, do all you desire to do, and have all you wish to have. You will be one step closer to mental mastery and your ultimate destiny. Because these laws are central to your happiness and well-being, it is important that you not only understand but also apply these basic principles.

As you read about each one of these four mental laws, ask yourself, "How can I apply this in my life?"

Δ *Thoughts are invisible forces.*

Δ *Living in harmony with mental laws creates a more balanced, peaceful life.*

Δ *Understand and apply the Four Laws of Mental Mastery – The Laws of Attraction, Expectations, Correspondence, and Cause and Effect.*

Law of Attraction

Every thought you entertain
is a force that goes out
and every thought comes back
laden with its kind.

RALPH WALDON TRINE

YOU ARE A MENTAL MAGNET!

Everything you have attracted in your life is primarily because of your thoughts. Your dominant thoughts create a "force field" of mental energy that radiates from you and attracts back into your life people and circumstances in harmony with these thoughts.

EMOTIONALIZED THOUGHTS

The power of this mental force field increases proportionately to the intensity that your thoughts are *emotionalized.*

Emotionalized means to make emotionally stronger. Whether it is a thought of fear or a thought of desire that is emotionalized, there is a definite result.

 Your thoughts, combined with your emotions radiating from you, create a powerful magnetic mental force field. This will attract back into your life people, situations, ideas, and opportunities consistent with your dominant thought.

The stronger the emotion you attach to a thought, the more rapidly you will attract people and circumstances in harmony with that thought into your life. This is why specific goals, with intense desires toward achievement, are vitally important to you. As a Power Thinker, get a vivid, emotionally charged picture of your desired goal. The Law of Attraction will inevitably bring into being the resources necessary to help you to achieve your desired outcome.

Tim is an acquaintance who is also on a personal growth journey. He wanted to get a better understanding of this "mental magnet" concept. He simply asked me, "What is the essence of the Law of Attraction?" I responded, "Essentially most aspects of your life – positive or negative – are of your own making. Your mental thoughts attract both good and bad into your life. The bottom line is, you want to attract a lot more good than bad."

Tim nodded his head indicating he understood what I had explained, thanked me, and was on his way.

As a Power Thinker, you must discipline yourself to focus on the thoughts of what you desire and want, not what you fear and don't want.

Δ You are a "mental magnet."

Δ Emotionalized thoughts increase your attracting forces.

Δ Specific goals with intense desire are powerful.

Law of Expectations

> *When you expect things to happen*
> *– strangely enough –*
> *they do happen.*

JOHN J. B. MORGAN AND EWING T. WEBB

YOU GET WHAT YOU EXPECT

The Law of Expectations simply states, "Whatever you confidently expect becomes your own reality." Your expectant thoughts become a self-fulfilling prophecy, positive or negative, depending on what you expect.

Power Thinkers exude an attitude of confident self-expectancy. They expect to be happy and healthy, they expect to be successful and wealthy, they expect to be cheerful and enthusiastic.

I was a senior at Islip High School in New York. We were playing for the league championship in basketball against our archrival Babylon High. Before the game I was confident we would win. It was a very competitive, hard-fought game. We were down by five points with twenty-seven seconds left – I still expected us to win. With twenty-one seconds left, I threw up a "prayer" while I was going out-of-bounds on the baseline. "Swish, nothing but net" – down by three points – I still expected us to win. I stole the in-bounds pass with sixteen seconds left and drove in for an uncontested lay-up – now down by only one point. Babylon High decided to call a time out and regroup. In our team huddle I shared my confidence that we were going to win this game.

Babylon in-bounded the ball and tried to run out the clock. With nine seconds left, I stole the ball from their leading scorer, dribbled the length of the court, and was fouled with one second remaining on the clock. It was a one-and-one situation, which meant if I made the first free throw the game was tied and I would get a second opportunity. If I missed, the game was over and we lost. There was definitely pressure – I was going to be either the "goat" or the "hero." Admittedly I was nervous, but I expected to make the free throws.

There were 1,500 spectators in the bleachers, and you could barely hear a pin drop. I took a deep breath, bounced the basketball a few times, and followed through as I released the free throw. Clank, as it hit the back of the rim; thud, as it banked off the backboard; and whoosh, as it dropped into the basket. The game was tied! The second free throw was good, we won the league championship, and I was carried off the basketball court by my teammates. The headlines on the sports page the next day read, "MAYER – ISLIP FREE-THROW HERO."

Against all odds, even down by five points with twenty-seven seconds left, I truly expected us to win. There is definitely power in the Law of Expectations when it is understood and applied.

EXTERNAL EXPECTATIONS

Throughout your life you are impacted not only by expectations of yourself, but also others' expectations of you – your parents, your boss, a significant other, friends, and co-workers. Hopefully all external expectations will be positive and supportive. But if not, understand that the expectations you have of yourself are in themselves powerful enough to override anyone else's negative expectations. You are in the driver's seat.

 Always expect the best of yourself, because you can never rise higher than the expectations you have of yourself.

Regarding your expectations of others, the same holds true. Your most effective motivational tool to inspire others is to continually and confidently expect the best from them. Your expectations exert a commanding invisible force that causes others to behave and circumstances to work out as you anticipate.

Positive Power Thinking, which was discussed in chapter three, is the Law of Expectations positively put into action. Remember, as a Positive Power Thinker, your most significant attribute is that you are **positively expectant** – you expect a positive outcome in advance.

Δ *Your expectant thoughts become a self-fulfilling prophecy.*

Δ *You get what you expect, so expect the best.*

Δ *Your positive expectations override the negativity of others.*

Law of Correspondence

*The greatest discovery of my generation
is that human beings can change
the outer aspects of their lives
by changing the inner attitudes
of their minds.*

WILLIAM JAMES

AS WITHIN, SO WITHOUT!

Your outer world mirrors your inner world. The Law of Correspondence simply states, "Everything that happens in your life outside of you **corresponds** with what is going on inside of you." Your outer world of manifestations corresponds directly with your inner world of thoughts and emotions.

Your outer world of people will correspond precisely with your own attitude. You will inevitably see your own attitude reflected back to you in the faces and reactions of people around you. If you have an upbeat, optimistic attitude, people will respond to you in a positive, cheerful manner.

Have you ever had a favorite waitress or waiter at a restaurant or coffee shop who really knew how to brighten your day? Heidi, a bubbly, outgoing sixty-two-year-old waitress at our local diner is just such a person. Sometimes just the sight of her will put a smile on my face. She always greets me with a warm, friendly hello. When I ask her how she is doing, she responds with a big grin and says, "If I felt any better, I think I might have to pinch myself!"

Heidi's outer world of happy customers corresponds directly with her optimistic, cheerful inner attitude. It is no coincidence that among all the waitresses she almost always makes the most tips. It pays to apply the Law of Correspondence.

Your outer world of relationships will mirror back to you exactly who you are – your true self. When you are happy, loving, and together, your relationships will be happy, loving, and harmonious. When your thoughts are of a troubled or negative nature, this will be reflected back to you in disruptive and unsettled relationships.

Your outer world of wealth and financial stability will correspond with your inner world of thought and preparation. Your prosperity consciousness will reflect itself in personal monetary gains.

CONTROL YOUR CONSCIOUS THOUGHTS

Regarding the Law of Correspondence, the only part of this principle that you have control over is in the area of your conscious thoughts. As a Power Thinker, you must therefore work toward your mental mastery by relentlessly filling your conscious mind with your desires of what you want in your life. Eventually your *outer* world will manifest an outcome that corresponds precisely with your *inner* conscious thoughts.

Δ *Your outer world mirrors your*
  inner world.

Δ *External manifestations correspond*
  with internal thoughts.

Δ *Control your conscious thoughts*
  to create your desired reality.

Law of Cause and Effect

What you sow, so shall you reap.

THE BIBLE

IRON LAW OF THE UNIVERSE

So important is the Law of Cause and Effect that it has been referred to as the Iron Law of the Universe. It basically says that there is a **specific cause** for every **effect** in your life. Effects are the conditions, circumstances, or results of specific causes. These include happiness and unhappiness, success and failure, and wealth and poverty.

If there are positive effects in your life that you wish to duplicate, simply trace them back to their causes and repeat the causes. If there are negative effects in your life that you want to eliminate, simply trace them back to their causes and eliminate the causes.

The beauty of this law is in its simplicity, but it must be applied to work. Rhonda, a chronic victim and unhappy soul, does not understand the Law of Cause and Effect. She continually thinks the same depressing thoughts (causes) day in and day out, year in and year out, and thus creates the same depressing results (effects) in her life. Her most often used depression-triggering question is, "Why did this have to happen to me?" The solution for Rhonda is to eliminate the causes that are creating the negative effects in her life. In this instance she needs to eliminate her disempowering questions and resulting depressing thoughts and replace them with empowering questions and more positive thoughts.

Charlie, on the other hand, is an optimistic, upbeat Power Thinker. He understands the invisible mental laws of the universe. His happy thoughts (causes) blossom into a happy and contented disposition (effects). Charlie's favorite happiness-triggering question is, "How can I make it fun?" The positive, happy results he gets in his life do not happen by accident. They occur by his application of the Law of Cause and Effect.

EFFECT ON HUMAN DESTINY

A Power Thinker's most significant distinction and application of the Law of Cause and Effect is that thoughts are causes and conditions are effects. Your thoughts are the main causes for the conditions in your life. Who you are now, and who you will become, is a result of what you think. Remember, "You become what you think about."

You have now come full circle in your personal growth journey through Power Thinking. You see, the Law of Cause and Effect is essentially the law of human destiny. This concurs with the book's central theme initiated in chapter one – "Control your thoughts (causes) and you will control your destiny (effects)."

Since then we have learned a lot about Power Thinking:

Δ   Everything in your life originates with a conscious or unconscious thought. The only thoughts you have control over are your conscious thoughts. Your conscious thoughts are controlled by the questions you ask yourself.

Δ   How you feel is determined by what you focus on. What you focus on is also determined by the questions that you ask yourself. If you want to feel better, then ask yourself better questions.

Δ   There is magic in asking the right questions. In fact, you can have almost anything you want in life if you ask yourself enough of the right questions. The right questions are the empowering ones. They will lead you to your desired outcome.

Δ   There are numerous empowering question-asking techniques that you can use to immediately improve your life. For example, the Five A's of Asking Awareness (Ask, Answer, Act, Acknowledge, and Adjust), Rate Your State, Morning Magic, and your Q&A Power-Thinking Pad.

Δ   Power Thinking is consistently asking yourself empowering questions, to control your conscious thoughts, to create the destiny you desire. There are at least thirteen types of Power Thinking. Each one has life-transforming potential when applied in your daily living.

Δ By consciously choosing better, more empowering words, you will inevitably improve your communication skills and enhance your chances of attaining the destiny you desire.

Δ Your beliefs significantly influence your decisions, which control and impact your emotions, actions, and future well-being. Therefore, it is imperative that you eliminate disempowering beliefs and reinforce empowering beliefs.

Δ Your thoughts are invisible, yet you do physically "reap what you sow" in your mind's garden. This manifests itself through your mental mastery in the destiny you create for yourself.

So be certain that when you design and shape your ultimate destiny, you not only *think*, but, more effectively, **Power Think!**

Remember to take the time to discover and apply the magic in asking the right questions. From this day forward, commit yourself to creating a day full of empowering questions. You will never – ever – regret it!

Good luck on your personal growth journey through Power Thinking.

Bill Mayer/Professional Speaker

Bill Mayer is available for

- *Keynote addresses*
- *Half-day seminars*
- *Full-day workshops*

For a biographical summary
and a list of speaking topics and fees,
contact Bill at

Tel 760 • 751 • 2798
Fax 760 • 751 • 2799

or
Bill Mayer International
11782 Alps Way
Escondido, CA 92026

The Magic in Asking the Right Questions
Book orders and success stories are also welcome.

Books – $15 each. Shipping – $3 first copy, $1 each additional copy.
Sales tax for California residents.
Make checks payable to Bill Mayer International.